L.A. INTERCHANGES

L.A. INTERCHANGES

A Brown & Queer Archival Memoir

LYDIA R. OTERO

PLANET EARTH PRESS

TUCSON, ARIZONA

Planet Earth Press
Tucson, Arizona
© 2023 Lydia R. Otero
planetearthpressaz.com

ISBN: 978-1-7341180-8-7 (paperback)
ISBN: 978-1-7341180-3-2 (ebook)

Cover photo © Laura Aguilar
Cover and interior design by Sara Thaxton

Library of Congress Cataloging-in-Publication Data
Names: Otero, Lydia R., author.
Title: L.A. interchanges : a brown & queer memoir / Lydia R. Otero.
Description: Tucson, AZ: Planet Earth Press, [2023]|Includes bibliographical
    references.
Identifiers: LCCN: 2023907155 | ISBN: 978-1-7341180-8-7 (paperback) |
    978-1-7341180-3-2 (ebook)
Subjects: LCSH Otero, Lydia R. | Los Angeles (Calif.)—Biography. | Sexual
    minorities—Biography. | Hispanic Americans—Biography. | Hispanic American
    families—California—Los Angeles. | Mexican Americans—Los Angeles—
    California—Social Conditions. | Los Angeles (Calif)—History—20th century. |
    BISAC BIOGRAPHY & AUTOBIOGRAPHY / Personal Memoirs | BIOGRAPHY
    & AUTOBIOGRAPHY / Cultural, Ethnic & Regional / Hispanic & Latino |
    BIOGRAPHY & AUTOBIOGRAPHY / LGBTQ+
Classification: LCC HQ76.25 O84 2023 | DDC 306.7/6/08968073/092—dc23

Dedicated to those who inspired me to think more critically and whose presence on this earth was unjustly cut short because of AIDS:

Valentino Sandoval
Ted Salaises
Michael Puente
Mark Kostopoulos
José Ramírez
Richard "Ricky" Coria
Joseph Domínquez
Abel Gutiérrez
Juan Carlos Rogers

"Definitions are vital starting points for the imagination. What we cannot imagine cannot come into being. A good definition marks our starting point and lets us know where we want to end up. As we move toward our desired destination we chart the journey, creating a map."

—bell hooks, *All About Love: New Visions*

CONTENTS

ILLUSTRATIONS

L.A. INTERCHANGES

Introduction

It is impossible to pinpoint when I fell in love with Los Angeles. An image of me at the beach while still in diapers hints that it happened early. The photograph captures a determined spirit who, despite shaky balance, continues to move forward seeking a modicum of independence. Growing up, I spent all my summers in Los Angeles with my maternal family. I understood that the city's vastness made it easy to get lost, but during my stays, I also picked up on its openness. The neighborhood kids I met and played with on the streets of Boyle Heights did not care where I came from, because many of them were from other places, too. I discerned the advantages a big city offered as my queerness began to bloom and my preference for boy's clothing and activities began to be scrutinized in my hometown of Tucson, Arizona. On a map, L.A.'s amalgamation of freeways resembled noodles; but on the ground, the distinctive neighborhoods, the faces of people of different ethnicities and races, and the gender outlaws that I spotted on the streets and buses all seemed to have a unique story to tell. Their stories, like my own, often centered on seeking second and third chances.

On a Saturday at the end of March, in 1978, after a devastating break-up and a failed attempt at college, I packed everything I owned into my blue Datsun and headed to Los Angeles. For four years after I graduated from high school, I had been mired in depression. My high school girlfriend had left to explore men, and I was not remotely close to completing my bachelor's degree, which added to my despair. I was stuck. I had always thought expressing my queerness would be easier in the City of Angels, but I had never mustered up the courage to move there.

FIGURE 1.1 Author at Santa Monica Beach, 1956. Private collection of author.

I had a major breakthrough the day before I left Arizona, though, thanks to a movie soundtrack. The highpoint of my life then was spending Saturdays at the movies. The advent of multiplex theaters made it possible to pay for one ticket, watch a film, then wander into another one. That Saturday, I sat through *Oh, God!* with George Burns, then slipped into *Looking for Mr. Goodbar.* Although I missed the first fifteen minutes, the trailers had led me to believe it celebrated a liberated woman who embraced her sexuality. But the film was disturbing, and the characters were troubled. Even so, the nightclub scenes and the soundtrack were alluring. About three-quarters of the way into the film, chills went through my body as Thelma Houston's soulful voice broke into "Don't Leave Me This Way":

Baby! My heart is full of love and desire for you!
Now come on down and do what you got to do.
You started this fire down in my soul.
Now can't you see it's burning out of control.

Houston's voice and tone, the song's beat, the lyrics and rhythm all mesmerized me. The way the song intensified and softened many times over filled me with unexpected emotion.

When the song was over, I was a different person. I stayed in my seat for a moment, stunned at what I had experienced and what I felt—an inner craving to be part of a crowd, on a dance floor large enough to hold many bodies, gyrating to music like the song I had just heard—a need to express locked-up desires by moving my body in a lit-up place where I could simultaneously disappear, see others, and be seen by others. More than anything, I wanted to celebrate my life.

Until then, I had resisted going to bars because I had not worked through the dreadful times when my father brought me to bars as a child. Going to a bar felt like moving backwards to me, but that afternoon, I longed for that indulgence. I knew it existed in Los Angeles, and I knew I had to find it.

I did not watch the rest of the film. I realized at that moment that I had waited too long to make my next move. I drove back to my small apartment, started packing, and called my mother to tell her I was leaving for

Los Angeles. To quash her concerns, I lied and told her there was a job lined up for me there. She encouraged me, probably because she had not witnessed excitement from me in a long time. Maybe she also knew Los Angeles offered her queer child more possibilities.

I fit all my belongings into my compact car and drove off at 2:00 a.m. with renewed resolve to love myself and enjoy my life. I had just turned 23 years old. By this time, I knew from experience that I could not separate my Brown self from my queer self. These interlocking pieces formed the core of my being. Although I did not immediately find Brown and queer groups, the time and place offered me the opportunity to meet others like myself.

After my queer cousin who I grew up idolizing unexpectedly passed on her apartment to me, I became an active member in Lesbians of Color (LOC) and the short-lived Lesbianas Latina Americanas. In the 1980s, I joined and eventually became a leader in Gay and Lesbian Latinos Unidos (GLLU). I was also a founding member of Lesbianas Unidas (LU).[1] Together we worked to create new spaces and expand the range of existing ones. GLLU jumped at the chance to support the endeavors of multiethnic or rainbow coalitions, but we never lost sight of the need to prioritize ourselves. As we met in our homes, typically small apartment rentals, we transformed them into sites that launched Brown and queer mobilizing, organizing, and socializing. In the latter part of the 1980s, I also stood with those who found themselves infected with HIV/AIDS and fought to ensure more services to battle the virus. Through GLLU, I played an active role in launching Bienestar, a community-based health-care and social services organization.

Ten years after I watched *Oh God!*, I was waiting for an elevator at Cedars-Sinai Hospital; when the door opened, the sole passenger, standing toward the back, was George Burns. Caught off guard, I said, "Hello, God." He responded by saying, "Hello, dear." I turned and held in my laughter as we both rode the elevator to our floor.

When I encountered Burns, I was as an electrician in L.A.'s Local 11 of the International Brotherhood of Electrical Workers (IBEW), there to update the emergency call system at the hospital. I was dressed in men's Levi's 501 jeans, a dark blue T-shirt, and work boots. I also wore a hard

FIGURE I.2 Author at Pride, 1987. Private collection of author.

hat, safety goggles, and a tool belt. I was covered in a slight layer of dust and carried a roll of metal-clad armored electrical cable on my shoulder. Despite these trappings, when I walked into the elevator, Burns quickly read the contours of my female body and referred to me as "dear."

Although much of this book will focus on my efforts as a Brown and queer community-builder in Los Angeles, I also used my body and physical labor to build the city. As an electrician during the 1980s, I was part of construction teams that built some of the most iconic buildings in Los Angeles, such as the Library Tower—now known as the U.S. Bank Tower and, at the time, the tallest building in Los Angeles—the dynamic Universal Studios' CityWalk, the 105 Freeway and the initial phases of the Metro Rail that now spans outward to the beaches and surrounding mountains. I also worked at some local film studios and took part in the Central Library renovation after fires in 1986 caused extensive damage.

As the opening paragraphs of this introduction make clear, my journey involved listening to popular cultural influences and the larger social
and political forces of the time. Born in Tucson, Arizona in 1955, I was
influenced by the optimism of the 1960s. In junior high school, learning
about the civil rights and women's liberation movements allowed me to
understand that a more just society and more expansive opportunities,
not available to my parents' generation, awaited Brown youth like me.

The earlier chapters in *L.A. Interchanges* address these idealizations
and how my relationship with my family nurtured my deep connection
with Los Angeles. I used my previous experiences of living in the city
with my Los Angeles family to anchor my new life here. The early chapters also provide insight into the evolution of my political consciousness.
Most personal histories of political transformation do not follow a linear
path. Mine certainly did not. When I moved to Los Angeles, I engaged in
relationships or employment that did not benefit me much but provided
me with opportunities to learn and to consider different options. I cannot stress enough how important it was for my personal development to
explore possibilities and to make what seemed like mistakes at the time.
Although I arrived yearning to meet and organize with Brown queers,
I needed to find them. This meant I needed to organize my life in a way
that made doing so a priority.

I currently identify as nonbinary. During most of my adulthood, society insisted on enforcing idealizations based on the existence of two
genders: women and men. Throughout *L.A. Interchanges*, I refer to myself as that assigned at birth, a female. In the 1980s, I fit however uncom-
fortably into the woman category, identified and organized as a lesbian.
I also base my decision to refer to myself, experiences and relationships
by the gender identities available during those decades to accentuate the
gender realities of the times. Like everything else, clothing was gendered,
and descriptors such as "men's clothing" are intended as a representation
of the time. I understand and respect why many nonbinary and trans
people have different relationships to their childhood and past identities than I have, and why, for example, some transmasculine people will
refer to experiences of their childhood self as a boy. As a Brown queer,
my evolving gender identity, experiences and its complexities are a vital
part of my story.

My memoir also offers a perspective of a Brown queer in the 1980s who intentionally did not seek community in a bar.[2] As I briefly mentioned earlier, unresolved childhood issues linked to bars influenced my perspective of that world. My father, Daniel, was active in the Veterans of Foreign Wars (VFW) post in Tucson and often volunteered to bartend at the club. Between the ages of eight and ten, despite my protests, I unwillingly accompanied him on his shifts as an unmonitored "volunteer" bartender. He should never have been allowed to tend to the bar. And, he should never have been allowed to take a child with him. Unfortunately, further lessons regarding alcohol dependency awaited me in Los Angeles.

Despite these experiences with alcohol, I became a social drinker and participated in bar culture by patronizing larger dance or disco clubs. I considered them sites of entertainment. Perhaps that is why I felt comfortable on dancefloors filled mostly with men. My quest to join and build alternative sites that made connecting with Brown queers outside of bars possible was motivated by my feminist leanings and knowing that I found women whose politics aligned with mine the ultimate aphrodisiac.

In 1998, I left L.A. and moved back to Tucson. On my visits to Los Angeles, I make it a point to drive by the buildings I helped construct. I sometimes ride the section of the Red Line Metro between Union Station and MacArthur Park to recall the months I spent beneath the streets installing the lights in the transit tunnel. Riding the train with friends allowed me to boast, "I built this!" And, on the way into and out of LAX Airport, when traveling underneath the Sepulveda Tunnel, I remind those friends kind enough to take me there that I installed the electric system that still lights it up.

About a few years ago, I went to Universal Studios by myself to see the fruits of my labor. I told the young person from whom I purchased my entrance ticket, "Twenty-five years ago, I was an electrician who worked on some of the rides and laid the underground electrical supply lines for CityWalk." She smiled and said, "That's so cool! I have never met anyone who helped build this place." I walked away feeling impressed with myself. Despite changes and upgrades, I was able to locate subpanels and electrical stations I had installed in the large amusement park.

> ***BAILE CELEBRANDO EL VERANO***, a Summer Celebration Dance co-sponsored by Connexxus Women's Center and Lesbianas Unidas of GLLU, features the music of Cheena, a no-host bar, prizes and a clean-and-sober section. Breakfast Club/Friendship Auditorium, Riverside Dr. & Los Feliz Blvd.; Fri., June 6, 8:30 p.m.-12:30 a.m.; $5. Call (213) 859-3960 or 391-5790.

FIGURE I.3 Advertisement of an event held at the Friendship Auditorium in *L.A. Weekly*, June 12, 1986, page 49.

FIGURE I.4 GLLU event held at Friendship Auditorium in 1982. Photograph by Louis Jacinto.

Plaques or dedications on buildings typically mention investment firms or philanthropists who funded their construction and the architects who designed them. The labor that went into their construction is systematically excluded. Although I do not have many photos of me working at the various construction sites, I carry many memories of my experiences as a tradesperson. Paystubs and other relevant documents that I have kept over the years also confirm the labor I invested in various construction projects that led to the existence of buildings or transportation systems that one can marvel at or travel today.

When in Los Angeles, I also visit meeting spaces or fundraising halls where Brown queers congregated and/or organized. For example, two organizations I was actively involved in, GLLU and LU, hosted a few fundraisers at the Friendship Auditorium on Riverside Drive near Griffith Park. When the thousands of people who attended events there drive past the large hall, I am sure that sometimes, memories of the music, dancing and maybe even the fundraising efforts they helped support flash through their minds. Like the buildings I wired as a tradesperson, no plaques or signage at the Friendship Auditorium provide direct evidence that Brown queers held events there or of the thousands who rallied to support their causes. Only story and voice can link memory to places.

During my time in Los Angeles, I squirreled away documents, as well as photographs of the Brown queer activists I worked alongside. Trained as a historian, I recognize that the date books, newsletters, meeting minutes, documents and photographs in my box are valuable primary documents. Each item provides direct evidence or personal testimony of an event or activity that took place during the 1980s. Thus, I refer to this book as an archival memoir because it is a documentation project. By integrating and building stories around the primary items in my collection, I am also activating them. *L.A. Interchanges* is a work of memory, but it is also a history. The inclusion of photographs also reminds me to focus on the everyday—that which I witnessed and participated in and which shaped my life a queer of color.[3] Not only do I have a box full of photos and documents I have carried for more than twenty years, but I am able to associate a memory with each item in that box.

When I embarked on this book, more than two decades had passed since I lived in L.A. The response to my 2019 book that centered on my childhood in Tucson, *In the Shadows of the Freeway: Growing Up Brown & Queer* has been encouraging and rewarding. I am proudest that my hometown library gave it a 2021 Southwest Book Award. *L.A. Interchanges* picks up where that book ended. As I dove into writing about my days in Los Angeles, it helped to remind myself that I was *not* writing a comprehensive history of queer organizations and recognized leaders. If names of people recognized in LGTBQIA+ circles as memorable leaders are not mentioned in this book, it is because they were outside the circles in which I traveled, organized, and socialized.

I have had to make some difficult decisions regarding what to include in this memoir. Much of what I write fits into the category of micro-activism or small actions that evidence the effectiveness of groups like GLLU to continually push boundaries. They also highlight a previously unacknowledged agenda to increase visibility and/or create new Brown queer spaces that prioritized Latine[4] issues and concerns.

In *L.A. Interchanges*, I center myself as I moved to different sites and engaged with different people in the city during the 1980s. Few of the people of color I organized or collaborated with have made it into history books, and the names of some of my young gay friends who died of AIDS oftentimes never made it into an obituary or AIDS quilt banner. But as my story unfolds, my aim is to portray queers of color as makers of history.

CHAPTER 1

Light on a Pathway

I am the Otero family's youngest child. I was born in 1955 in Tucson, Arizona. Out of five children, I am the only child my mother gave birth to in a hospital. My father, Daniel, was born in 1911, a year before Arizona achieved statehood. My mother, Cruz, was born in 1913. Friends and family called her Chita.

My mother's pregnancy with me was marked by stress. At forty-two, she was much older than the average mother. Chita felt embarrassed by her pregnancy, because it signaled to the world that she was still having sex, and she stopped attending social events. She gave birth to me on Valentine's Day and named me Lydia, after Lydia Mendoza, an acclaimed ranchera/Tejana singer my parents admired. My siblings and I were closest to my mother's side of the family, and we were raised alongside dozens of cousins. My mother's closest companions were her sisters.

My family ties to Los Angeles began in the early 1930s, when my grandfather, Fernando Otero, moved his family of eight there during the Great Depression to find work. Unfortunately, Fernando died in L.A. in 1937. On my mother's side, my grandmother's sister Christina Delgado moved to L.A. after World War II. She was born in Tucson in 1906, and was Chita's nina, or godmother.

Christina bought a large house on Boulder Street in Boyle Heights, east of downtown Los Angeles. She had two apartments in the back of the house, and she paved the way for two of my mother's married younger sisters, Mincy Lopez and Elodia Hernandez, to move there in the late 1950s. When they moved to Los Angeles, they both got menial jobs at different chicken-processing plants. It was before mechanical killing and

FIGURE 1.1 Author's mother Cruz and four of her six sisters, around 1942 in Tucson. Back row, left to right: Elodia, Margarita, Cruz ("Chita") and Maria Luisa ("Licha"); front: Armida ("Mincy") Private collection of author.

defeathering machines were introduced, but even this work was better than the opportunities back home.

Once her sisters moved to Los Angeles, Chita started making regular trips there with her children in tow. My father never came on these trips. My home in Tucson was isolated, with unpaved streets and few neighbors; L.A.'s lively urban scene could not have been more different. There were restaurants and stores—lots of them—only five blocks from Christina's house on Brooklyn Boulevard, now César Chávez Boulevard, which was always bustling with activity. On weekends, the family went to Disneyland, Knott's Berry Farm, Redondo Beach, or the Pike in Long Beach for outings. On weekday mornings, I watched cartoons and children's shows that were not available in Tucson, like *Bozo the Clown*, and tagged along with adults taking the bus to the Central Market downtown for fresh vegetables and meats for dinner. The days flew by in Los Angeles. Each one brought a new adventure. And I discovered a kindred queer spirit there in my cousin, Connie Haro.

My tía Mincy lived on Christina's property in a small one-bedroom apartment in the back. Growing up, I spent most of my summers with Mincy and her husband Mando. My mother, Chita, stayed a few weeks at the beginning of summer, then left me with her sister until the end of July. I would return to Tucson just in time to shop for school clothes.

Around 1962, when I was seven, tía Mincy secured a "better" job manufacturing curtains. That summer, when she got home from work in the early afternoon, she moved through the house in slow motion. It caught my attention and drew my focus away from the television. I would watch as she shushed me quietly, her finger over her mouth, and made her way gingerly behind a screen in a corner of the dining room. She would undress carefully and put her clothes in a bag.

She worked with fiberglass at the curtain factory, and she did not want to expose us to it. Tía Elodia also moved on to a new job, but the two sisters did not remain close. Only when my grandmother, my mother, or their other sisters visited L.A. did they spend time together.

I always volunteered to pick up things we needed at the corner market, something we could not do in my barrio back home. Sometimes, when Mincy was at work or busy baking, I walked to a store further away, on Mott and Folsom Streets, seeking more adventure. Kids my age gathered outside that store, and I got to know a few.

Every summer, especially when I was younger, I looked for Geneva. She was my age, and stayed with her grandmother for a few weeks in the summer, too. Quick-witted, shorter, and browner than me, she once blurted out, "I don't like boys." I was stunned but retorted, "I don't either." In typical Geneva fashion, she said, "I know." It was 1963. I was eight, and it was the first time I used my voice to publicly affirm my queerness. Over the years, I lost track of Geneva and even forgot her name, but I always cherished that moment. It made me feel less alone to know that she too, and maybe others, belonged to a similar Brown queer family.

I took long naps while watching television, and I savored the breezes floating in through the windows. Back home, I lived near the I-10 freeway, which dominated and drowned out other noises, so the sounds I heard through my window in L.A. captivated me. I most appreciated the birds chirping and singing. It might have been why my mother always had pet birds in our house. She gave them French names like Pierre and Michelle, and she loved hearing them sing. When I came back to Tucson in the fall, adjusting to the high-decibel drone of the freeway always took a while.

There was a large washroom as you entered the back apartment, and windows had been added to the screened-in porch. During the summer, Mincy put a foldaway cot out there and called it my room. I often went to bed early during the summers in Los Angeles, just to lie on my bed and listen to the sounds outside my window. Our neighbors to the left and right, the Kobayashis and Nakaharas, were Japanese American, and I would try to make out their conversations. Tía Christina told me both families were assigned to live in internment camps during World War II. Although the younger family members spoke English, the older generations spoke Japanese. It was enchanting to listen to. The biggest treat was being awakened by the matriarch's getas, or wooden shoes, when she walked on the back patio.

Our Japanese American neighbors must have come to expect my arrival each summer, because they sometimes caught me parting the hedge or standing on something to get a glimpse of their yard. It was unlike anything I had ever seen in the desert. The greenery in the Kobayashis' courtyard looked like a nursery. They even had a pond. A few times, I watched an elderly woman in a beautiful kimono dancing on the patio while music spilled out of the house.

Tía Christina's house was rather grand. It was built in 1912, and the walls were covered with real wood, not the thinner fake paneling popular in the 1970s. Elaborate moldings lined the house, hinting at a more storied past—until she started adding magazine cuttings and flowers brought home from weddings to the wall décor. In the late 1930s and early 1940s, a Jewish American medical doctor lived there. The Keenbergs owned the house in the 1950s, before Christina bought it; the patriarch of their family had immigrated from Russia. In an assessment of Boyle Heights, historian George Sanchez illuminates its history of "sustained interaction across racial and ethnic groups." His argument that "newcomers learned the meaning of American identity, through their integration with others from different backgrounds" refers to earlier decades, but during my summer stays, I learned to appreciate the multiethnic, multiracial mix that L.A. offered and my hometown did not.[1]

When I was growing up in Tucson, the vast majority of people I knew were of Mexican descent, with a sprinkling of Chinese and African American. I never met anyone who identified as Jewish, Armenian, or Filipino. From films like *West Side Story*, I knew a lot of Puerto Ricans lived in New York City, but I had never met any Brown people who did not identify as having Mexican roots. At my high school, even those Mexicans and Mexican Americans brought up outside the Catholic Church raised eyebrows for being different. The only white people I knew were teachers and school administrators.

In 1978, when I drove up to my tía Christina's house, Boyle Heights was changing. One of the Japanese American neighbors had moved away, and the neighborhood was becoming less diverse and more brown. The morning I arrived, I parked my car, looked up at the house, and walked up the stairs to the front door. I felt comfortable enough to arrive unannounced.

When my tía opened the door, she enthusiastically shouted one of my family nicknames through the screen door. "Lily!" We hugged and I immediately announced, "I am moving here!" She sat me on the couch and took a more serious tone. "Does Chita know?" I hedged the truth a bit. "Yes. She knows, and she is excited about it." Her second question was, "Do you have a job?" I said no but I was going to start looking. Before we moved to the kitchen, she made a quick call to my cousin Connie. "Aquí está la Lily. Dice que se va a mudar para vivir aquí." Connie must have said that she would be right over, because that was the extent of the call.

My tía gave me an earful of family news. Most troubling for her was that Mincy and Mando had moved away. Christina lamented that she felt helpless to stop them. My mother had already filled me in on the falling out, but their parting felt strange to me too.

My cousin Connie arrived half an hour later and declared she always knew I would end up in Los Angeles. "I just expected you a lot sooner," she said. Connie was Christina's grandchild. She was born in 1944, and Christina raised her as her own. How and why this happened seemed like a nonissue growing up. Connie and Christina were extremely close, and Christina doted on and pampered Connie by buying her a number of sports cars.

Connie always dressed in men's clothing. She visited Tucson often and brought her girlfriends, who were sometimes not much older than me. When we sat around the dining room, I made sure to sit next to them and marvel at their beauty up close. Connie brought new partners often, but she definitely had a type—pretty, petite, long-haired Mexicana or Chicana femmes.

Although my mother never warned me to stay away from Connie, and no one in our family ever said a negative word about her, but not

FIGURE 1.2 Connie during the summer of 1967 in Boyle Heights. Photograph by author.

talking about our queerness was not the same as acceptance. When I was twelve, my mother told me privately, "I know what you are." Her tone was hushed. She was standing in the shade, watching me walk on a short brick wall in our side yard. "You talk about girlfriends, but you never talk about boys," she said. "If you decide to be that way, then you will have to leave. It will be too hard for you if you stay." I did not have the words to respond. In hindsight, I see that I charted the course of my life around my mother's outline of my limited options as a queer. At an early age, I knew that if I wanted to live "that way," I needed to leave Tucson.[2]

When I was about twelve years old and Connie was twenty-four, we bonded as kindred queer spirits. She was quite charming, with a great smile that showcased her huge dimples. During the summer of 1967, when I was eleven and in L.A. for the summer, she let me tag along on errands and the occasional excursion. We never gave our queerness a name or talked about how our desires made us different from other people.

Sometimes, during my summer stays, some of Connie's friends would come over to party in her bedroom and listen to records. That summer, Connie drove a cool Pontiac GTO with bucket seats and a gear shifter on the floor. We cruised Sunset Boulevard with her friends a couple of times and drove up to the Griffith Park Observatory to gaze at the city lights below, while they clowned around and, often drank alcohol. Being around Connie and her friends gave me a glimpse into Brown queer lives.

The day I arrived in Los Angeles, both Connie and I assumed I would stay with her. I drove behind her to her apartment in Alhambra, about eight miles east of downtown L.A. in the San Gabriel Valley. She lived in a yellow building at the end of South Stoneman Avenue, a street lined with small houses with nicely kept lawns. Up one flight of stairs sat a one-bedroom apartment, #C, which I would get to know well. I heard the familiar noise of traffic as soon as we arrived. The San Bernardino Freeway, the I-10, was less than 30 feet away, and a brick wall separated the apartment from the train tracks. When the train swept past, the whole apartment trembled. The screech of metal wheels on metal tracks took some getting used to.

Connie helped me carry my few belongings upstairs. We put them in the corner, and I dropped myself on the couch, knowing it would be my

FIGURE 1.3 Apartment building on Stoneman Avenue in Alhambra, 2022. Photograph by author.

new bed for a while. Connie went to the fridge and came back with two beers. "You go ahead," I said. I took the liberty of asking about some of her old girlfriends, but Connie turned on an old black-and-white television and lost interest in talking. Something was off. Turning down the beer had upset her.

I had not slept in over 36 hours, and eventually, I dozed off. I woke up suddenly a few hours later when the train went by. At first, I thought it was an earthquake. I could see through the window that it was dark. Connie still sat on the opposite end of the couch, and a few empty beer cans lined the coffee table. "Do you want a beer now?" she asked optimistically. "No, but I am hungry." Connie put her hands in the air and said, "You'll need to get something." "Okay," I replied, "Let's go somewhere!" "I am not hungry," Connie said curtly.

I remembered there was a Circle K a block away on Garfield Avenue, the closest main street, and decided to walk there. I took my time, stocking up on enough chips and sweets to share with Connie. When I returned, she had put a pillow and a light blanket on the couch and retreated to her bedroom. I watched TV and ate my snacks in silence, feeling like a burden.

The next day, I got up early. I had always been an early riser. I packed some clothes and the notebook I jotted phone numbers in and snuck quietly out of the apartment. I bought a Coke at the Circle K and called my tía Mincy from the payphone. She was surprised to hear I was in Los Angeles, and gave me directions to her new house, a small two-bedroom on Whiteside Street in City Terrace, east of downtown L.A. Despite the street name, only working-class Brown people lived there, in small houses in much poorer shape than the one in Boyle Heights.

Connie's apartment was on one side of the I-10, and Mincy's was on the other. From Mincy's backyard, you could look down and see all the busy lanes of the highway. No wall separated the homes from the freeway, but at least the train tracks were on the opposite side. Mincy's backyard also had a view of the hills. When night fell, the lights sparkled off to the east. My aunt called the view Mexican Beverly Hills.

Mincy smiled and danced in place when she saw me. I can see her exuberant smile to this day. Her husband Mando had already left—he worked as a construction laborer—and she fixed me a huge breakfast with pancakes, not from a box but from scratch. It was like old times. Mincy loved telling elaborate stories, and I loved to listen and ask questions. We called my mother, then Mincy ironed my clothes while I took a shower. She offered me some words of encouragement before I left to see my tía Christina, who had promised to save the Sunday want ads for me.

The first question tía Christina asked was if Connie had gone to work. She worked the night shift, and her schedule required working Sunday nights. I said, "I don't know," but Connie had still been in bed when I left that morning. Tía made a "humph," retrieved the newspaper for me, and brought me her push-button phone with the long cord.

Before I left for Los Angeles, I worked part time at a bank processing center. They trained me as a ten-key data entry operator. Before electronic scanners, when someone cashed a check, someone else—an actual human—had to read the numbers and type them into a number pad, so a machine could encode the check's value at the bottom. My title was proof operator, because I proofed checks.

I turned out to be good at this tedious job, so much so that they offered me a full-time position. I turned it down, afraid it would interfere with skipping classes, eating junk food, and watching reruns of *Gilligan's Island*, *The Munsters*, and other mindless television. But it was miraculous how my fingers moved so quickly, punching in numbers microseconds after my eyes and mind together deciphered the amounts. Even sloppy or cryptic writing became clear to me.

There were a number of help-wanted ads for proof operators in the *L.A. Times*. I zeroed in on the Security Pacific ad, drawn by its byline: *Bank on a Career with a Future*. I called the number, and the woman asked if I had experience and how fast I could proof. She also asked where I was from and if I had graduated high school. We talked for a while, and I gave her my tía Christina's number. When we hung up, I felt glad that I at least had a marketable skill.

I decided to take a walk to the corner store before making more calls. All of Boulder Street, and the store too, awoke so many memories, and I took my time on the walk back. As I was coming back to the house, drinking a Coke, I saw tía Christina standing on the porch looking out for me. "Lily!" she said. "The bank called and they want you to call back." We were both excited, and she watched as I called the bank back. The number was for the manager at a branch in Temple City, further east in the Greater San Gabriel Valley. The bank manager asked about my proofing experience and where I was from, too. It made me think that maybe my impression was right—that people who lived in L.A. assumed everyone was from someplace else. She asked if I could be at the branch at 2:00. I wrote down the address, and tía Christina predicted, "You are going to get the job."

I asked her if she knew how to get to Temple City, and she said, "Call Connie." Luckily, she answered the phone and offered precise directions. I asked if she would be home that evening, and Connie said she needed to leave for work at 8:00. "I'll be there before then," I said.

I walked into the bank a few minutes before 2:00, and the manager got up to welcome me. She was not much older than I was, and she seemed comfortable being the boss. She walked me over to the proof machine in the back, near the vault. "It's exactly like the one I used at my last job," I told her. I filled out some paperwork, and although she did not guarantee me the job, she said to expect a call from her later in the day. I returned to tía Christina's house to tell her about the interview, and the branch manager called while I was still there. She wanted to hire me! She told me I had to go through a two-day training, gave me the address, and emphasized that I needed to be there at 9:00 o'clock on Thursday morning.

In less than a day, I had gotten a job! I called Mincy and had dinner with her and Mando, as I had done so many times growing up. When she brought out a Snickers bar cut in three pieces for sharing, I knew we were celebrating. This was one of their favorite desserts, one that Mincy served often during the summer when I lived with them.

I was anxious when I returned to Connie's, because I did not have a key. She left a little later for her nightshift job. The rest of the week, I left early so she could sleep late, and I only saw her for a few minutes before she left for work.

On Thursday, I showed up at the Security Pacific on 6th and Alvarado, southwest of downtown Los Angeles. It was kitty corner from MacArthur Park. My family had picnicked there when I was younger, and I always enjoyed seeing the city center's skyline in the near distance. Donna Summer had a pop hit about the park around this time, and hearing it on the radio always made me nostalgic for running around the park and riding small boats in the lake as a kid. I parked in the bank's lot and walked to the corner to look at the park.

An older, professionally dressed white woman approached me and asked, "Are you Lydia?" She told me she would be supervising me for the next two days. We waited outside for the other trainee, who showed up ten minutes late. She wore a leather jacket and rode a motorcycle. I could see my supervisor's distaste; it lingered for the next two days, while she praised me a bit too excessively.

During lunch breaks, I walked around and explored MacArthur Park. The drug hustling was undeniable, but I also saw Brown folks simply enjoying being outside, sitting on benches feeding birds and talking to each other, even though the lake had been drained. Awkwardly, I struck up a conversation in Spanish with a middle-aged woman who lived in the area. She told me that when the lake was drained a few months ago, many relics and treasures were found at the bottom.

She had recently emigrated from Nicaragua, she said, and had moved because President Anastasio Somoza had made life in her country intolerable. Her son had been caught up in the violence; now, he was dead. She called it terrorism. Protests against Somoza had been staged at the park, she told me. Despite experiencing such devastation, she radiated warmth and kindness. I left feeling deep compassion for her.

As I walked back to the bank, I thought about my old insecurities around speaking Spanish. In public school, I learned it was not safe to speak Spanish in certain spaces. My elementary school considered it a deficiency. A monitor once pulled me off the playground to scold me for it. "You know you are not supposed to speak Spanish," she said. She brought me to the principal, who stood over me, pointed to a chair, and declared loudly, "I want you to sit here and think about what you've done!" I sat for hours, feeling ashamed of who I was and where I came from, just as the education system intended.

Growing up, I only spoke Spanish with close family members, and I would clam up in situations where I felt judged or unsafe. At the same time, I knew most people out in the world expected me to speak Spanish because of how I looked. I felt confident when speaking English, and I considered it my first language, but as I returned to the bank, I realized that I had just had a meaningful exchange with a stranger, exclusively in Spanish. "Maybe I was much more bilingual than I gave myself credit for?" I reasoned. I did not speak fluently with the Nicaraguan woman at the park. I stumbled often, but she understood, and we communicated successfully.

As I crossed the street and looked around, it hit me that I now lived in Los Angeles, and I was sure to encounter more monolingual Spanish speakers. I took my conversation in the park as a sign. It was time to be different and put aside feeling inept at speaking Spanish. I strutted a bit as I embraced my newfound pride in my Spanish-speaking skills. I felt like I had let go of a small piece of emotional baggage and had located somewhere inside me a skill that allowed me to relate to people who looked like me—people who, like me, had come to L.A. to start a new life.

The need to connect played an important part in my decision to move to Los Angeles. I loved that a simple walk through the park resulted in such a profound experience. I started to pay more attention, and I

FIGURE 1.4 Protest against U.S. government intervention in El Salvador and in support of the El Salvadorian struggle at MacArthur Park. Photograph by author, 1980.

learned more about the conditions forcing Nicaraguans and other Central Americans to move to the U.S. I could not have predicted then that, in the upcoming years, I would participate in several protests for immigrant rights at MacArthur Park, and I could not have foretold that, in 1991, thirteen years later, I would be installing the lighting at the Westlake/MacArthur Park Station on the Red Line Metro Rail. I worked in a dark, dank underground tunnel for about a month, climbing up a thin metal ladder during my lunch breaks to be outdoors again and people-watch. Unfortunately, I could not enjoy the lake, because it had once again been drained. Inevitably, I thought about the Nicaraguan woman I met when I first moved to Los Angeles, who had influenced my life in ways she would never know.

After lunch on our last day, my fellow trainee was late again. The supervisor berated her again for wearing a "man's" leather jacket and because "women should not ride motorcycles." The trainee often blamed her boyfriend for her tardiness, and that last afternoon, the supervisor said, "I bet she doesn't even have a boyfriend." Emboldened by my experience at the park, I attempted to "out" myself in L.A. for the first time. It did not go so well. "I don't have a boyfriend," I offered. The supervisor refused to head down that rabbit-hole. "But you don't drive a motorcycle," she said. "Let's get back to work."

Coming out to people in different situations was difficult. Most people saw what they wanted to, and I had not mastered how to make the statement clear. Like other queer people of the time, I had to find my own way of coming out. My clothing would be central to that script.

Clothing is such an important aspect of expressing one's identity. All queers have benefitted from the gender outlaws before them, those who pushed boundaries and suffered the consequences. Born in 1932, Nancy Valverde from East L.A. pushed those boundaries by wearing men's clothes. She was arrested several times in the late 1940s and early 1950s. The L.A. Police Department charged her with "masquerading," and she was sentenced to up to three months in jail. Although the police eventually stopped arresting Valverde, they continued to harass her.[3]

My cousin Connie, born twelve years after Nancy, wore men's clothes. To my knowledge, she was never arrested for doing so, but her career options were limited. Connie worked lower-tier factory jobs all of her life.

I only started feeling comfortable with having my photo taken in the last fifteen years, because I have let myself dress in a way that expresses myself more fully. From the time I entered elementary school in 1961 until I graduated high school in 1973, school dress codes required me to wear dresses. Finding more masculine dresses and shoes was hard, but I put a lot of effort into it—even if I was the only one who could see those qualities in my choices.

Even today, I do not wear men's clothes. Instead, I seek out what I consider to be the most masculine looking clothes in the women's department. They fit my body better, and I appreciate the aesthetic. Over the last half century, I refined a look that feels like mine, even if it evolved from an oppressive place.

In 1978, I did not look queer to most people. At twenty-three, I was, in a way, attractive. Although I always wore pants, I preferred tighter-fitting clothes, which accentuated my curves, and I wore a longish hairstyle, as did most men at the time. I knew I was escaping a stigma that other, more masculine women could not. Inside, I was gender nonconforming. Outwardly, I looked to most people like a woman of the time—a time when androgyny and fashions we now consider outrageous were in vogue.

It took decades for me to recognize that for most of my life, I had been emulating male celebrities and role models. As a child, I wanted to be like my brother-in-law Raul. Some people called him Elvis, and he idolized Presley. I did too. Later, in the late 1960s, I wanted to be like Paul McCartney. In the early 1970s, in my high-school art class, I drew a pencil and charcoal portrait of Tom Jones, the Welsh singer, and taped it over my bed. My mother encouraged the fascination with this hypermasculine singer. Jones had his own television show, and his swaggering renditions of "She's a Lady" and other hits allowed me to secretly feed my growing lust for women.

> Well, she's all you'd ever want.
> She's the kind I like to flaunt and take to dinner.
> Well she always knows her place.
> She's got style, she's got grace, she's a winner.

Now, I shudder at these chauvinistic lyrics, but when I was fifteen, they captured my inner desires to be with women and have women find me attractive. My mother saw the drawing as proof of my attraction to Jones, and she approved of my art because of it, but the creative force inspiring me was wanting to be Tom Jones. I was attracted to many female celebrities, like Natalie Wood and Marianne Faithful. I drew them too, but I did not dare put them up in my room.

When Cat Stevens released *Tea for the Tillerman* in late 1970, all my other male role models fell by the wayside. I spent hours listening to his music and looking at his photograph on the back of the album cover. I used to rationalize that I was attracted to men who projected femininity; it allowed me to avoid confronting my desire to emulate their look or be them. In the 1980s, I fashioned my style around the various characters John Travolta played, especially Tony Manero, Danny Zuko, and even

Bud Davis. I was poised and ready for the even bigger blown-out hair styles, including perms and mullets.

My first week in Los Angeles, I had not been able to spend much time with Connie, and I looked forward to Friday evening because she had the night off. Two of her friends, who also dressed in men's clothes, came over and started drinking. I had a beer with them, but I did not have much to add to the conversation. When I mentioned my efforts to learn more about Los Angeles, one of Connie's friends said, "I'll show you L.A."

The way she said it made it sound like she was hitting on me. Even Connie picked up on it, and surprised me by saying, "My cousin is not going to go with you. She is a prude."

The comment stung. I had never been called a prude before, but at the moment I felt like one. I asked the others if they were going out or to a bar, because I wanted to check out their scene, but Connie said, "No. We are having fun here." It turned into a long night, and I eventually grew weary of their banter and dozed off on the edge of the couch. Connie told me to go sleep in her bed, but I felt anxious and did not feel comfortable with her friends.

The next morning, I slipped away to Mincy's for breakfast. As I washed the dishes, I asked her if I could move in with her. She instantly said "Yes," that we were family and that she and Mando both enjoyed having me around. I felt a huge relief, because around her, I felt appreciated and loved.

I returned to Connie's that Saturday afternoon and told her I was going to live with Mincy. Connie did not try to dissuade me. "Do what you want," she said, and went back to bed while I gathered my things. I had idealized Connie's life when I was growing up. In Tucson, I had seen her drink at parties, but I never thought alcohol might be a problem for her. My infatuation with a lifestyle that included bringing a new girlfriend to Tucson every time she visited had distracted me from looking deeper. Because of our age difference, I had expected Connie would want to take care of me. Maybe she expected the same from me.

I was a part of a wave of queers moving to large urban cities. Scholars call it the Great Gay Migration of the 1970s and early 1980s, when tens of thousands LGTBQ+ individuals across the U.S. moved to metropolitan areas to find community and be more whole.[4] Most struggled more than I did to gain a foothold in the city. In the twenty years I lived in Los Angeles, I had ten different addresses, but when I arrived, I had places to stay and access to a phone number where employers could return my calls. I also had an informed perspective regarding the city's streets and layout, and my tía Mincy, who had taken meticulous and loving care of me all my life, would continue to do so once I moved to Los Angeles.

I was friendly, and I did my job diligently at the Temple City bank. I did not have contact with the public, so I did not feel pressured to dress up. I owned one pair of navy-blue polyester-blend bellbottom pants and two button-down tops that I switched up, and every day I wore a long sweater that covered most of my body. My salary was about $146.00 a week, and I prioritized saving for an apartment. Investing in a new wardrobe was low on my list of things to do.

Every workday, I picked up checks to proof from a Mexican American loan officer named Norma. She was in her mid-forties, but she looked older, and she would often talk to me about making "the right" decisions in life. She talked a lot, but I let her—I saw it as a way for her to control the conversation.

Norma never married. She lived with her mother. I knew straight women like her in Tucson, women who did not venture far from their families, went to church each Sunday, and dedicated themselves to their jobs and family. Norma had worked at the bank since she graduated from high school. I admired her steadiness, but I knew I would never take her advice.

One day, Norma showed up with a large shopping bag. "This is for you," she said. In the bag were two pairs of polyester-blend pants. "You can wear them to work," Norma said. The first question that popped into my mind was, "How did she know my size?" I briefly considered not accepting the clothes, but the new clothes meant a lot to Norma. She smiled every time she saw me in the new pants, although I never disguised my lack of desire to move up the professional ladder.

In time, Emily, the other Mexican American who worked a desk job at the bank, befriended me as well. She was 35, recently divorced and unhappy about it. She also wanted to make up for a decade of feeling trapped in her marriage. Emily started inviting me to have lunch with her at the Crest, a bar and grill across the parking lot from the bank. It had low lighting and booths. It felt like restaurants I had seen in old movies. I would order a well-done hamburger with extra pickles and a Coke, and Emily would down two Bloody Marys.

Sometimes the white middle-aged male loan officer she thought was hot would join us. Emily told me they were having an affair, and she swore me to secrecy, but of course everybody knew about it already. I told Emily that I was queer, but she brushed it off and said her sister was the same way. She preferred talking about how much she hated her former husband and about all the sex she was having now that she was single.

When I lived with Mincy and Mando, I did not feel free to explore my queerness. They had both known I was queer since I was a child. Everyone in my family knew, even if they did not discuss it—when I was just six years old, my older brother nicknamed me Butch. I spent my weekdays at work, and during the evenings, I watched television with Mincy and Mando, despite disliking some of Mando's choices—shows like the *Dukes of Hazzard* and *CHiPS*, with lots of car chases and macho personalities. I paid them $40.00 a week for room and board. On the weekends, I took Mincy or my tía Christina shopping or out for errands. Out of respect for Mincy and Mando, I never stayed out late.

Because I had not made friends or considered bars an option, I mostly drove up to and around Hollywood during my time off. Bookstores were one of my favorite destinations. I picked up free queer newspapers, hoping they would inform my future explorations, but most of the free publications were intended for gay men. Their advertisements accented white male penises, or cock shots, and their want ads were primarily for hooking-up for sex.

I found the portrayal of unbridled gay male sexuality fascinating, and my eye found the glossy color images of men's bodies alluring. To me,

they represented a group of people with their own code and way of doing things that I did not know. I never felt the urge to explore this world
sexually, but I wanted to know it. The imagery also reminded me of why
I loved disco.

I often went to the library and checked out books. Most of the few
books I owned were left behind in Arizona. Only a tattered copy of Dee
Brown's *Bury My Heart at Wounded Knee* survived the move.

Once I was in Los Angeles, I purchased a copy of *Our Right to Love: A
Lesbian Resource Book*.[5] I had high hopes for the book, but although it was
innovative, I did not really connect with the content. It was too white, too
East-coast. I understood the significance of "our right to love," but there
was nothing about dancing or connecting in ways I perceived as fun.

I had always identified as a feminist, but in my women's studies class in
college, I experienced a gulf between myself and white feminists. I found
them patronizing and racist. Sometimes they would talk across me, as if I
were not there, or chuckle outwardly when I spoke. When I pointed out
issues of race and Virginia Wolfe's class privilege, they could not contain
their hostility, and I ended up dropping the course.

I appreciated that *Our Right to Love* discussed lesbian sex so openly,
but I mostly ended up looking at the photographs. I left my two books
and a growing pile of gay magazines under my bed. I knew Mincy, a
cleanliness fanatic, looked through them when I was at work, but we
never talked about them.

The one magazine I paid a dollar for and read cover to cover was
the *Lesbian Tide: A Feminist Lesbian Publication, Written by and for the
Rising Tide of Women Today*. I had read a few copies at the library in
Arizona. Printed on newsprint, it was more than forty pages of articles,
current events, interviews, book reviews and opinions on issues such as
coming out, being single, lesbian rights and building a national lesbian
movement. The *Tide* also tended to focus on L.A. matters.[6]

In addition to the content, I took note of the *Tide*'s writing collective.
I assumed Jeanne Cordova was a Chicana, although she did not seem
to align with that identity in her essays. She represented a rare potential
Brown role model for me, and I kept a watchful eye on her. *Our Right to
Love* featured a photograph of the *Tide* collective or staff, and one of the

Members of The Lesbian Tide Collective: Sharon McDonald, Shirl Buss, and Jeanne Cordova

FIGURE 1.5 National Gay Task Force and Ginny Vida, eds., *Our Right to Love: A Lesbian Resource Book* (Englewood Cliffs, New Jersey: Prentice-Hall, 1978), 249. Courtesy of Ginny Vida.

writers, Shirl Buss drew my attention. I never would have predicted that a few years later, I would get to know and love her.

When I started working at the bank, I opened my first checking account. Mincy and Mando paid all their expenses, including utilities and rent, in cash. One day, Mincy asked if I could cash Mando's paycheck. "I probably can," I said, and she handed me the check. The check was for an unusually large amount, and I asked, "Is this for two weeks?" "No," she said. "It's for one week." I was shocked that Mando, a laborer in the construction industry, made such a high wage. He undoubtedly worked hard—he came home tired, and his clothes were covered with odd smudges. Sometimes he even smelled like gasoline or random chemicals. The first thing he did when he got home was step into a hot bath that Mincy had waiting for him.

Mando's paycheck opened up a whole new world of unions and blue-collar work for me. I attributed his wages to the local laborers union, of which he was a member. If I were in a union, I would earn as much as men did. I also loved working with my hands. When I was younger, I was my brother-in-law's shadow and loved helping him fix cars, evaporative coolers, and washing machines; dig new trenches for sewer, gas, or water lines; and help install the underground pipes. Becoming a laborer did not appeal to me because I wanted to use hand and power tools; it was learning a trade, making a good wage in a job that mandated wearing boots and jeans. It seemed like a dream come true.

The next weekend, I went to the local library and looked through some literature on the construction trades. I read about the various blue-collar professions, such as plumbers and sheet-metal and iron workers. One had to be accepted into and enter an apprentice program to learn the trade through classes and on the job training.

Eventually, I encountered a line in a construction-trade pamphlet that said something like, "Of all the trades, electricians earn the highest hourly wages, but they require all applicants to pass an Algebra exam before they will consider them suitable for apprenticeship." I was so glad that I had been one of those geeks who loved math. I closed the pamphlet and returned all the materials I had checked out to the librarian. I had found my answer: I was going to be an electrician.

That Monday, I called the International Brotherhood of Electrical Workers (IBEW) Local 11 to ask about their apprentice program. Yes, they said, you fill out an application—that included a copy of high school transcripts confirming I took two semesters of algebra—and take a math test. Unfortunately, they only offered the exam on alternate years. For the first time in my life, I felt headed in a positive career direction. It did not feel like destiny, but more like a light on a pathway previously shrouded in darkness.

Although I knew times were changing, I did not expect the Local 11 representatives I talked to on the phone and in person to be so welcoming. Tío Mando on the other hand felt women should not be construction workers. I defended my decision and reminded him that he often asked for my help when replacing cabinets and repairing plumbing, and that he asked me to climb up trees to trim the high branches with his reciprocating saw while he stayed on the ground and collected the branches that fell.

He remained steadfast and instructed Mincy to dissuade me, because the men on the job sites would make my life hell. She dutifully promised that she would try. Mincy shared his concerns over lunch at a coffee shop inside a Thrifty Drugstore, but ended up giving me more treasured advice. Neither of us shared it with Mando. "He does not want you to do this," she said, "but I do. Why shouldn't you make as much money as him, or more even?" She lamented the lack of opportunities and low-paying jobs available to her during her lifetime. "If I could have been an electrician when I was younger," she said, "I would have done it."

In 1977, about a year before I began looking into an apprenticeship, the U.S. Department of Labor started requiring trade unions and construction contractors who worked on federal projects or received federal funds to hire women. The department had already instituted regulations for the inclusion of African Americans and other minority groups, but the League of Women Voters Education Fund and a few other groups had filed a lawsuit to ensure that women were also allowed entry into the construction trades. A study indicated that women carpenters, electricians, painters, plumbers, machinists, mechanics, and workers in a few other skilled trades made up less than 1–3 percent of the nation's 11 million skilled blue-collar workers.

Mando's closed and sexist attitudes reflected the entire construction industry. The Buildings Trade Council of the AFL-CIO initially opposed the new regulations, saying they did want another "quota" imposed or affirmative action regulation.[7] When I called about joining the electricians trade union, they were in the midst of change, because the federal government also funded their apprenticeship program.

About two months after I moved in with Mincy, Connie called and asked to speak with me. Connie told me she was moving and asked if I wanted to take over the lease for her apartment in Alhambra. The rent was $250.00 a month and was paid until the 15th, so I needed to move in right away. I also needed to pay a deposit. Connie gave me the number of the landlord's daughter, who lived in a large two-bedroom in the building and was expecting me to call. She told me to bring a money order with me when I moved in on the 15th. It was that easy. Apartment #C was furnished, which made it an even a better deal.

When I arrived to pick up the key and move in, there was no trace of Connie. For the first few weeks, I slept in my clothes on the bare mattress because I could not afford bedding, and I continued to have dinner with Mincy and Mando.

I wish I could say things worked out for the best with Connie, but they did not. I often asked my tía Christina to have Connie call me, but I never saw her again. Mincy and Mando moved back to Tucson in 1982, and Christina and Connie moved to Las Vegas around the same time. When my tía Christina died in 1986, everyone in my immediate family lost touch with Connie. My tía Elodia remained in Los Angeles, and I visited with her every once in a long while, but I no longer had Mincy to watch over me and comfort me. By that time, however, after a few relationship blunders, luck had brought me a partner who felt like family and encouraged my personal growth.

Learning the Richness of Queer Culture

My second-story apartment in Alhambra proved the ideal place to continue building a queer life for myself. It was close to Mincy's and to all my different jobs. I knew the city's layout and could maneuver the streets and neighborhoods east of downtown pretty well. When I got lost, I relied on the downtown skyline to find my bearings. I had a terrible sense of direction, and still do. When the smog made downtown impossible to see, I realized I needed to invest in a map, but getting lost seemed part of an agreement I had made with the city.

Global tensions, especially in the Middle East, and the surging demand for oil caused severe automobile fuel shortages in the late 1970s. Prices doubled. In 1973, when I graduated from high school, gas cost 39 cents a gallon. By 1979, the price had risen to 86 cents a gallon. Having a car meant I could survive in Los Angeles, but like most people who lived in the automobile-oriented city, I was dependent on fossil fuels. Because gas was in such short supply, California began a rationing system. The last number of your car's license plate determined which days you could get gasoline. Luckily, my apartment was about two blocks from a gas station on Garfield Avenue, diagonally across from the Circle K. Cars lined up before the gas station opened. When I was low on gas, I parked my car in the line the evening before, locked it up, and went home. I woke up before the gas station opened the next morning and only sat in my car for about ten minutes. Most people, many of them women with children, slept in their car in a line that stretched around a number of blocks.

Within a few months after I got my own place, I dabbled with some ill-fated relationships, but joining a political support group called Lesbians of Color (LOC) proved my most impactful involvement. When I had first moved to Los Angeles, I prioritized soaking in all the Hollywood glamor the city had to offer, and I continued to dedicate Saturday afternoons to the movies. The Egyptian Theatre on Hollywood Boulevard, built in the 1920s, was my favorite. Colossal columns stood at the entrance to the movie theatre, and Egyptian-style paintings and hieroglyphs covered its walls.[1]

But in 1980, a year after I joined LOC, I was part of a contingent that marched down Hollywood Boulevard, pumping my fists and decrying violence against women. My affiliation with this group allowed me to venture into spaces and discussions I had longed to enter, and it made me aware of what was possible. The friendships I made in LOC led to weekend nights at discotheques, but equally important, they led me to experience shared spaces where people of color rejoiced in their queerness. I was becoming the person I always wanted to be. As long as I could make my rent, what I did for a living did not matter much while I awaited a call from the IBEW Local 11.

In August, after about five months at Temple City, Security Pacific Bank consolidated their branch proofing departments and reassigned me to their downtown headquarters. I felt relieved, because I knew too much about the people I worked with, and my bank manager had started expressing interest in me. She waited to walk me to my car after work and reached for my hand a few times. Although her eyes sparkled and she had a nice smile, I had sense enough to know that a married woman with two children and carrying her third was too complicated for me. The fact that she was the most powerful person at the bank branch intrigued me, however. She wore a lot of thick gold jewelry and moved in a world of privilege that I did not know and found alluring. Her husband owned a successful business, and she could afford manicured nails and dresses made of delicate fabrics. On my last day at the branch, the tellers and other staff arranged a going away party for me at the Crest. I never said goodbye to the bank manager, but she sent me a card a few months later, professing her love for me. She included a photo of her new child.

My job moved to a huge processing center in a 55-story skyscraper at 333 South Hope Street in downtown L.A. It served as the headquarters for the Security Pacific National Bank; today, it is the Bank of America Center. I worked the swing shift, from 3:00 to 11:00 pm. For the last few months of 1978, it was the perfect job for me. Some nights, after getting off work, I drove north on the 101 Freeway to cruise Sunset Boulevard in Hollywood and drive by iconic buildings like the Cinerama Dome movie theater and the Capital Records Tower, which was associated with the Beatles, with the Hollywood sign in the distance. Before the monster developments of today, independent businesses lining the street either painted their storefronts or wove unique design elements into them to attract attention, creating a fascinating eclectic urban fabric in the process. In late 1978, businesses associated with old Hollywood, such a Schwab's Pharmacy and Dino's Lounge, remained open.

Unlike the bank branch in Temple City, where it seemed people actively engaged in silencing or suppressing my queerness, my new job site was a queer mecca. Most of the hundred or so people who worked in the processing center were around my age, and my coworkers were mostly Brown or Black, with a sprinkling of Filipinas. The office occupied one huge floor lined with four small offices, with glass windows on the right side. The top supervisor was an older gay white man, and the junior supervisors were all straight African American women. I was assigned a machine in the second row of about 35 proof machines, towards the front entrance.

There were only a handful of white males on the floor. Upon my arrival, I was assigned to one of them, Nick. He was flamboyant and tall, and his walk and manner of speaking ensured that everyone knew he was gay. Nick was responsible for training new employees. He sat next to me for the next week and inundated me with information about the gay scene. He appreciated when I showed interest and asked for more details—which I often did, especially about gay male sexual practices. Although he was white, he exclusively desired Latinos as romantic and sexual partners. He told me why and what bars he frequented to meet them. When I shared that I wanted to meet more Latinas like me, Nick said, "I can tell you are not femme" and warned me that I looked too straight. He suggested I change my look, starting with cutting my hair. I had gotten a glimpse into the butch and femme scene through my cousin Connie, and when I expressed that I did not want to be part of that scene, he said rather sarcastically, "Then girl, you are in a lot of trouble." I found it easy to dismiss his assertion, because the fact that I existed meant others like me did too. My task was to find them.

Up to this point, Nick was the first person in L.A. that I had talked openly with about being queer. I took some of what he shared with a grain of salt. After all, he was a white guy, but the fact that he was so way out and immersed in being a gay man impressed me. It helped me realize that being queer was not just about knowing where to hang out, the dress codes, and the rituals: queerness was a culture, a way of living.

Nick also shared gossip about the people we worked with, and took the liberty of telling everyone I was a dyke. Being outed this way was new for me. It made me feel exposed and vulnerable at first, but I appreciated being called a "dyke." It seemed direct, and I preferred it more than the label "lesbian." Although few at the check-processing center seemed to care, I often looked for evidence of disapproval. I found it in Amelia, a Mexicana who made it a point to refer to me as "basura" (trash) every time I walked by her station. Four years later, I saw Amelia making out with another woman at a house party, and I made sure she saw me when she came up for air. I wanted to confront her physically, but instead I stood back and watched as shock transformed her face. She looked down immediately and pulled away from the woman she had been kissing. No blows or words were exchanged, but my body trembled with anger as I left the party and walked to my car.

Most of the people in that huge check-processing center were interesting in their own way. Every day, I made it a point to meet my required output early so I could walk around and talk to them. Each person had a story about living in a different part of L.A. Levi was the hippest; he moonlighted on the weekends as a dancer for *Soul Train*, a popular televised African American dance and entertainment show filmed in L.A. I looked for him during breaks because he liked to share celebrity gossip. In his world, everyone was gay, and I soaked up everything he said. Each of his tidbits held a nugget of truth, or at least I thought they did, and I

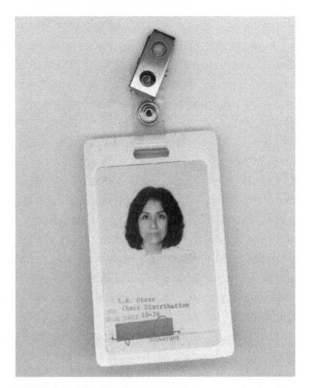

FIGURE 2.1 Check processing center security badge, 1979. Private collection of author.

tried to get more information by asking questions like, "Before Chaka Khan and Natalie Cole became lovers, did they have other girlfriends?"

Randy, an African American man who sang in his church choir, took a zealous interest in my gender identity. I "read" him as gay, but he claimed he was not. He was about a year younger than me and challenged my queerness often, saying things like, "You are not a dyke." Being publicly outed was new, but quarreling about my queerness was novel too. I never thought I would declare, "I AM a dyke!" so affirmatively and so soon after arriving in Los Angeles. I mention this because Randy, like so many others, was voicing the need for new labels to identify people who did not fit the old ones as queerness became more public.

But Randy had reason to question my queerness. About two weeks after I started at the downtown processing center, Carl joined us. He was white and about two years younger than me, with a German-sounding last name that I have since forgotten. He had dirty blond hair with loose curls that he left unattended. He looked like pop singer Andy Gibb. He had been born and raised in Downey, a city southeast of Los Angeles, and he and his parents were friends with the singing group the Carpenters, who had a number of pop hits when I was in high school. I knew the words to most of their songs, and I prized the group's drummer and lead singer, Karen Carpenter.[2] Carl did not have much facial hair, and was handsome in a feminine way. One day, he said, "My mother made me an extra sandwich. You want one?" True today as it was then, the direct line to my attention is through food.

I met Carl in the garage, and we ate our sandwiches in his light blue Volkswagen Karmann Ghia. His mother started making me a sandwich daily, and after we ate, Carl would drive his car sharply around corners in the empty garage floors. He made the tires squeal and I would hang on. He had heard the rumors about me and said he did not care. He had a knack for detaching himself from what went on at the check-processing center, especially from Nick's advances. During our ten-minute breaks, Carl immersed himself in a book instead of socializing.

One day after we ate our sandwiches, Carl asked, "You wanna kiss?" I moved toward him and it was nice. He liked using the word "great," so of course he said, "That was great." We never talked on the phone or saw each other outside work, but we frequently made out in his car after lunch. One day, on our way to the elevator, he pulled me toward him gently, and we kissed standing up. Reality hit when I felt his hard penis against me. At that moment, I realized that moving forward meant complicating my life in ways I had never envisioned. Carl and I never ate lunch together again. Everything continued to be "great," and life in the processing center full of hormonally charged young people moved forward. Carl stands out because this was the most intimacy I ever experienced with a man.

I had a more dramatic liaison a few weeks later, with a low-level supervisor who always looked at me when she walked past. She worked in "return items," where they tended to damaged checks that would not run through the system. I glanced at her and always looked away, but she never did. She often wore fitted pantsuits, blouses with large collars open almost to her breast line, and a gold chain. I found her attractive the moment I saw her. At some point, I asked the straight Latino guys at the loading dock about her. In many ways, they were bigger gossips than Nick. They had noticed her too, and one said, "Es muy atractiva." After they teased me about asking about her, they told me she was married and had a child, but they did not know her name. They referred to her as "Pepsi," because she was the color of Pepsi Cola. I thought she was out of my league. After all, I was still wearing the pants Norma had given me.

One day, she stopped and leaned into my proof machine. She looked directly at me and said, "I hear you are one of them." I did not know what to say. "Don't be shy about it," she kiddingly said in what I thought sounded like a Texas accent. "You want to go to lunch tomorrow?" I squeaked out a "yeah," and she said, "Meet me at the parking lot at 6:30." She winked, turned, and left. I watched as she walked away. So did everyone else near me, in disbelief. I looked over at the loading dock guys, and even they looked shocked. The next morning, I fought the temptation to buy new clothes. "It is only lunch," I told myself. "Do not make such a big deal about it."

We met at the elevators, and she nodded for me to follow her. She drove a newer Mercury Cougar, which only made me feel more like I was out of her league. "You like tacos?" she asked. "Yea," I replied. I breathed out a quiet sigh of relief at the thought of tacos. I sat back, got comfortable in the luscious velour passenger seat, and looked outside. She drove to the Los Burritos taco stand on Echo Park Boulevard, about two miles away. "I'll pay," she said, handing me a $10 bill, "but you go order and get our food." We both had three tacos and a Coke. She instructed me to put the change in the console holder and warned me not to drop any food in her car. We ate our tacos quickly and in relative silence, because we only had thirty minutes for lunch. As I exited the car, she complained I slammed her door too hard and told me not to do it again.

I would learn more about this taciturn woman as our taco excursions continued. Her name was Joan, and she had been raised in South Central Los Angeles.[3] Her son was around five months old when we met. We also started meeting after work, which meant close to midnight, to "talk" on a side street west of the 110 Freeway. I parked my B-210 behind her and jumped into her car. Our talks became make-out sessions, and I began visiting her at home, where we had sex. The problem was not only that she was married, but that her husband Henry was a police officer.

Although we were close in age, Joan seemed to be more of an adult than I was. Like most people, she needed to juggle the contradictions life threw her way, but she did not seem in a rush to change anything. I found the contradictions more troubling. Joan loved the financial security and luxuries that Henry provided, and she loved being a mother and wife. She and her family were active members in a Holiness Pentecostal Church. A few times, Joan played a cassette of church sermons for me in the car. Listening to them made me uneasy, and I would insist she play the cassette with the song "I Just Wanna Stop" by Gino Vannelli, which I was into at that time, and reminded me of our make-out sessions.

I assumed that I was Joan's first "lesbian" relationship, but to my surprise, I learned there had been a few. She sometimes wore a pin on her lapel that looked like a little mouse; it turned out she had gotten it from frequenting Vermie's, a lesbian hangout in Pasadena. Vermie's gained more attention in the 1980s, when the singer Melissa Etheridge was discovered there.[4] I shared with Joan that I had started attending Lesbians of Color (LOC) meetings on Sunday afternoons, but I stopped trying to explain why the group appealed to me when she dismissively remarked, "I'd rather go to a bar to meet women and talk." Joan's dismissiveness offended me, but I also liked our arrangement. She dedicated the weekends to her husband, family, and church while I went out with the new friends I was making through the LOC support group.

At least twice a week, I arrived at her house at around 10:00 in the morning to spend time with her and watch the soap opera *All My Children*. I had sometimes watched the show with my mother and sisters, so the characters in Pine Valley were familiar to me. I typically left Joan's house around 1:00 pm, caught a nap at home, and got ready for work. Once, I stayed too long and bumped into her husband, in full police uniform, as I was leaving. Tall and strong-looking, Henry also wore a holster with a gun.

Other than fast-food excursions, we only went out together in public once, at the end of 1978. Joan bought us tickets to see Teddy Pendergrass at the Greek Theatre. He was an R&B Soul singer with a deep manly voice and was loaded with sex appeal. I was not a huge fan, but I enjoyed Teddy's music, especially "Wake up Everybody," which had been released a few years earlier and had a social justice focus. After that night, I became a fervent fan.

It was the first time I attended an event at the Greek Theatre. I had walked the outside of the amphitheater with my family as a child but had never been inside. It was gorgeous! When Joan and I reached the entrance, I remarked, "Wow. There's a lot of women here." Joan said there was supposed be. "It's a women's only concert." I was amazed. I had read about women only events in the *Tide*. Those gatherings were making a political statement, but Pendergrass used "women only" to enhance his artistic and commercial appeal. Today, we would call it his "brand." The audience was mostly African American women, with a sprinkling of Latinas. The few straight men in attendance were accompanied by women, and I spotted a number of gay men who seemed extra jubilant to be there.

Our seats were near the stage. Once Teddy appeared, women flooded the stage and aisles. Of course, he played up his deep voice, seductive lyrics, and hypermasculinity. For a moment, it had felt cold outside at the Greek, but all the heat generated by enthusiastic women made it feel hot. Alcohol was being passed from person to person, and Joan and I took a couple of swigs of what I assumed was whiskey, although I had never tasted whiskey. The crowd's intensity that evening made me think, "This must have been what it was like to see the Beatles in the 1960s or Elvis in the 1950s."[5] The crowd went ballistic when he took off his shirt. Even I was seduced, and I screamed at the top of my lungs. I could not get enough of him. Of course, I did not desire his sexy sweaty body—I wanted to *be* Teddy.

It surprised me that Joan knew most of the women around us. She kept saying, "This is Lydia" and introduced me as her friend. I was the only one who was not Black in that section. Joan and I hugged a couple of times, but jubilant fans around us were dancing and hugging us and each other throughout the show. A well-dressed woman two seats down from us reached her arm out, pulled me close, and kissed me on the lips. I considered it part of the fun, but Joan quickly pulled me away.

After the concert, Joan drove us to a diner where we met many of the women who had been at the concert. The woman who kissed me showed up too, and it became one big party again. Many of them wore wedding rings, and I assumed they passed as straight out in the world. I later asked Joan if she knew the women who sat near us at the concert. "Some," she answered. By then I had learned that she often shrugged off questions she did not want to answer. But clearly, this group of African American women knew each other well. It awed me that they had found each other and formed their own network.

As a related aside, in 1986, a friend invited me to a club near downtown where, other than me and a handful of others, all of the patrons were well-off Asian and Asian American women, mostly Filipinas. They were dressed in formal attire and wore coordinated white outfits. I stood outside watching—or maybe I was gawking—at those arriving by limousine. By then, I knew a few out Asian American queer activists, but they were not representative of the women I saw that night. The fifty or more women who walked into the club all seemed to know each other through a network they had created to ensure their privacy and exclusivity. I learned that they met at different clubs on random Saturdays. They must have formed an elaborate phone tree to keep up with everyone. I never saw the friend who invited me again, and I never again had the opportunity to witness this type of gathering. Even as I write about that night, it seems like a fantasy. The existence of these clandestine groups and gatherings, including Joan's and Connie's networks of friends, represent the many pathways that connected queers in Los Angeles.

Joan's efforts to stay in the closet started to bring up old feelings and resentments for me. My previous two-year adult relationship, with a woman I had met in high school, ended with her saying, "I am not like you"—meaning I was queer and she was not. Breaking up with her and knowing she started seeing men made me feel like I had fallen down a dark hole and been left behind. On the other hand, the world seemed to reward her for moving forward, embracing her straightness, and disasso-

ciating from me. The final straw with Joan came when she suggested that
I start getting close to Carl again as a smokescreen for our relationship.

After I had been on the job for a few months, Nick was promoted and
I was offered his job. This meant I got to train all the new employees and
enjoyed a little bump in salary to $165 a week. I celebrated by buying new
clothes. Things seemed to be coming together. I had also met someone
in LOC that I found attractive. I wanted to feel unencumbered to start
dating, but I felt I needed to end things with Joan first.

It was hard to fully separate from Joan when we saw each other at
work. Early Saturday evening, the week after we broke up, she paid a
surprise visit to my apartment. She had never before bothered to come
to Alhambra to see me. Luckily, I was alone. I let her in, but I could not
wait for her to leave. The thought "What if her husband followed her?"
kept running through my mind, as did the fear that he would barge into
my apartment seeking vengeance.

Joan's visit left me feeling rattled, and I learned that mixing work and
pleasure came at a price. Despite the promotion, after Joan showed up at
my apartment unannounced, I quit my job at Security Pacific. I got a job
at another check-processing center, of which there were many. At that
point, my social life had expanded to include the women I was meeting
through LOC, whom I found much more exciting and interesting than
those I met at work.

In the summer of 1979, an announcement in the *Tide's* "L.A. Calendar"
section alerted me that Lesbians of Color (LOC) met on Sundays at
5 PM. The notice was a gateway to a community of like-minded queers.
I felt like I had been preparing my entire life to be a part of a group like
LOC. It became the core political social group through which I made
new friends and alliances for the next three years.

The meetings were held at the Alcoholism Center for Women (ACW),
about five blocks south of MacArthur Park. The group met in one of the
larger rooms on the first floor, to the right of the Tudor-style building's
entry door. In addition to folding chairs, the room had a few upholstered
armchairs, two larger couches, and a piano. A large window lit up the

L.A. Calendar

REGULAR EVENTS

IMRU GAY RADIO: KPFK 90.7 FM every Sunday, 8:30 p.m.

SPELL CASTING CLASS: Every Sunday 3-5 p.m. Feminist Wicca, 442 Lincoln Blvd., $3.00 donation. Call 399-3919.

LESBIANS OF COLOR: Alcoholism Center for Women, 1147 S. Alvarado, L.A. Every Sunday 5:00 p.m. Call 869-4730.

RADICAL THERAPY: Open group, Womonspace, 237 Hill St., Santa Monica, every Thursday 7:00 p.m. $2.00 donation for unemployed, $5.00 for employed, but no womon turned away for lack of funds. Call 396-0054.

"ANNU'S IN OUR IMAGE": Clayworks, every Thursday 7 to 10 p.m. Feminist Wicca, 442 Lincoln Blvd., Call 399-3919.

FIGURE 2.2 Announcement in *Tide*, July/August 1979, page 29. Courtesy of Lynn H. Ballen.

room. A few times, people entering the ACW peered in, and when a certain older African American woman attended meetings, she insisted on drawing the curtains. This made the room feel dreary, but I understood how curtains added an additional layer of protection for some.

Only about eight women, all African American, attended my first LOC meeting in August 1979. They all knew each other, and no one tried to make me feel welcome. This was not how I had envisioned my first meeting. To make myself feel better, I reasoned it was some sort of protective mechanism—that they were cautious about opening themselves up to people who might never show up again. At that meeting, a few of them shared that a large number of women had marched in the LOC contingent at the L.A. Pride Parade the previous month, on July 1st. It was the 9th time the annual event had been held in Los Angeles.[6]

In 1979, LOC opened the parade, marching down Santa Monica Boulevard. It marked the first time a contingent of lesbians of color participated in the event.[7] In a movement led exclusively by whites, and in a parade that glorified white male bodies, I could sense that the women who had marched felt proud about openly proclaiming a place for lesbians of color. I, too, was excited to learn about the march, although I felt disappointed that I had not known about it earlier. I had been in L.A. for more than a year, all the while oblivious to the queers of color who were meeting and marching. I was irritated with myself for wasting so much time.

Despite feeling a bit unwelcome at my first meeting, I made it a point to be early for the next one. I really had no other choice. At that time, LOC was the only way to integrate myself into that network in Los Angeles. The next week, the same sprinkling of women attended, but one woman, Renée, smiled at me.

I shared many similarities with the women who made it to the Sunday meetings. Some had attended college and were interested in social issues and resistance movements. We were all challenging, in our own ways, the social expectation to be straight. Embracing our multiple identities or intersectionality was not easy then, and it remains difficult. The vast majority of the people in LOC were in their mid to late twenties and worked in lower white-collar professions. Like me, most were looking for alternatives to bars for meeting friends. A few, like Renée, took the bus to the meetings and found others like me who were more than willing to give them a ride home.

Renée lived with her parents in Baldwin Hills. In the late 1970s, media representations of more affluent middle-class African Americans who lived in large houses with elaborate driveways never appeared on television. When I dropped her off at her home, I asked, "Is this where you live?" "Where did you expect me to live?" she asked. I replied, "I don't know? But not here." Renée shook her head and got out of the car. Despite my ignorance, she and I spent hours on the phone and started dating.

Lesbians of Color was a relatively new group. It had been established a little over a year before I started attending the meetings. Its founders had participated in the National Lesbian Feminist Organization (NLFO), which had formed in March of 1978. Before that, no national organization of lesbians existed. Although the NLFO set ambitious goals, it did not last more than a year. In an unprecedented move, NLFO had devised an inclusive organizational structure from its inception to address the racism in the white lesbian movement. After contentious debates and processing, the organization moved to ensure that 50 percent of the decision-making positions and steering committees would be comprised of women of color.[8]

It is clear that lesbians of color in Los Angeles were invested in the organization. After the NFLO's initial meeting, they continued to meet twice a month in their private homes, "discussing projects and doing circles where we share feelings, dreams, experiences etc." Whether the lesbians of color formed the new group, Lesbians of Color, as a recruit-

Women of color meet twice a month in LA. We meet at one another's houses and
spend time recruiting members, discussing projects and doing circles where we
share feelings, dreams, experiences etc. So our communication mailing address
is: POBox 149 Pasadena, CA 91102 contact: dah dah, flying clouds, gladys.

FIGURE 2.3 Handout "Information on the women of color caucus in los angeles
has been doing publicly—" dated April 28, 1978. IN "LOC LA" File, ONE Institute, Los Angeles.

ment strategy to bring more women into the NLFO or sought to organize
separately from white lesbians is unclear. Either way, the LOC group in
L.A. continued to meet after the national group disbanded.[9]

One issue came up often when I was first attending LOC around 1979 to
1980: the Navy was trying to purge lesbians from the USS Norton Sound
in nearby Long Beach.[10] In this homophobic sweep, African Americans
were disproportionally accused of being lesbians. An ACLU representative attended a LOC meeting, and a few members, including the woman
who insisted on closing the curtains, attended some rallies and reported
back. The ACLU mainly sought to denounce the tactics used to gather
the evidence to indict the women of lesbianism. It seemed unjust and
complicated. The accused were not seeking to come out as queer or
have the liberty to serve in the armed forces as lesbians, but the racism
was so pronounced that it demanded denouncing. When the investiga-
tions ended, the majority of women purged from the Navy were African
American.

Although LOC's existence was certainly political, the group left little
in the way of records. Flyers and announcements advertising events and
workshops can currently be accessed in queer archives, but LOC never
drew up agendas or even sign-in sheets during its heyday. When matters
regarding supporting an issue came up, women raised their hands, but
their votes were never recorded in the form of minutes. The group did
not elect officers. Instead, those present drove the impromptu agenda
by bringing up things they wanted to talk about. Women dropped in
and out because at its core, LOC was a support group. The personal
was political, and the group provided a space for us focus on our issues.
Sometimes, someone would announce a protest and invite LOC to par-

ticipate, but the group rarely organized it. LOC's loose structure made it easy for individuals to claim to represent LOC in the larger community, but that did not necessarily mean the group had discussed and approved the matter. Looking back, I would surmise that although I was active in LOC, I could never be considered a member, because such a category did not exist.

In 1979, LOC staged a protest at the Palms, a lesbian bar on Santa Monica Boulevard in what is now known as the City of West Hollywood. On Sunday, November 18, a few African American women went to the Palms after a LOC meeting. They were asked to show three pieces of identification to be served. Usually, the bar required only one major identification card, such as a driver's license. The request for multiple forms of identification was a clear indication the Palms staff sought to exclude people of color and cultivate a white lesbian clientele instead.

The women in LOC organized against this injustice, and about twenty-five of them and their supporters staged a protest at the Palms the next month. I was visiting family in Tucson at the time and did not attend the protest. At the next meeting, I listened to those who reported that, as they carried picket signs and marched on the sidewalk in front of the bar, people in passing cars yelled out "dykes" and hurled racial slurs at them. They also reported that the management was hostile and unrepentant.[11]

LESBIANS de of COLOR

LESBIANAS DE COLOR/LESBIANS OF COLOR/LESBIANAS DE COLOR/LESBIANAS DE COLOR

The Lesbians of Color Caucus was formed to meet the needs of asian,black, latina,native and other lesbians identified as wimin of color. LOC was formed to facilitate personal, social, cultural and political growth of its members. LOC was formed to maximize our effectiveness in the wimin's community.LOC is dedicated to fighting against all forms of opression. Lesbians of Color meet on the first and third Sunday of the month at 1147 S. Alvarado, Los Angeles at 5pm. All Lesbians of Color are welcome. Contacts: Dah Dah 388-2708, Alicia 392-7090, Flying Clouds 746-7209. Messages Noon-6pm Oak 399-3919. LOC Box 149 Pasadena, Ca. 91102

Lesbianas de Color fué formada para responder a las necesidades y realizar las metas de lesbianas asiáticas, negras, latinas, nativas y otras lesbia-nas identificadas como mujeres de color. LDC fue formada para facilitar nuestro desarollo personal,social, cultural y político. LDC fue establecida para asegurar nuestra influencia en la comunidad de mujeres. LDC estan de-dicadas a la lucha contra opresión de cualquiera clase. LDC se reunen el primer y tercer Domingo del mes en 1147 S. Alvarado, Los Angeles a las 5pm. Todas las Lesbianas de Color estan invitadas. Mas información: Alicia 392-7090, Yolanda 449-3271 LDC Caja Postal #149 Pasadena, Ca. 91102.

FIGURE 2.4 Early LOC Flyer, 1979. Private collection of author.

The local *Lesbian News* published a short piece two months after the protest as a result of a press release that someone affiliated with LOC had sent to them. Typically, they did not cover these types of events. The short article ended by reporting that "Lesbians of Color is requesting the community boycott the Palms."[12] Around that time, I never patronized the bar, so I cannot say the boycott hurt their business, but the fact that LOC took a stand on the issue remains impressive. I did go to the Palms a few times after 1987, because by then the bar had tried to mend its relationship with patrons of color by holding Salsa and Hip-Hop nights. The place was packed on those nights. Sadly, though, the Palms, the last lesbian bar in West Hollywood, closed in 2013.[13]

The next year, on May 19, 1980, LOC took a public position against rape culture, domestic violence, and all forms of violence against women. They participated in the "Take Back the Night" march, which drew attention to the fact that women could not safely walk down the street at night in Los Angeles. At that time, organizers of the march claimed L.A. was "the rape capital of the world."[14] At the LOC meeting before the march, an important voice in the group, Linda Lucas, reminded us of the Los Angeles Police Department's (LAPD) role in perpetrating violence against women. The previous year, two officers had opened fire on and killed thirty-nine-year-old Eula Mae Love (also known as Eulia Mae Love) after a confrontation with gas employees who had come to shut off her gas. LAPD exonerated the officers, who had shot Love twelve times at close range under the pretense of self-defense.[15] In fact, a coalition to establish a Citizens Police Review Board had been initiated about six months before the Take Back the Night march, with Linda Lucas representing LOC and participating in a few community discussions backing the initiative.

More than a thousand people marched that Saturday night in 1980. I waited with a few others from the group at the corner of Highland Avenue, until the procession turned left and headed east on Hollywood Boulevard. We jumped in when the LOC banner reached us. I felt like I was having an out-of-body experience as I marched down the middle of Hollywood Boulevard with a rambunctious group of women of color chanting, "Hey, hey, ho, ho, the patriarchy has got to go!" and "No more battery! No more rape! No more woman hate!" Someone gave me a can-

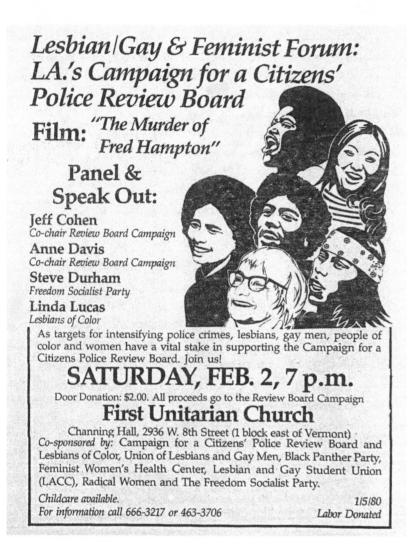

Lesbian/Gay & Feminist Forum: LA.'s Campaign for a Citizens' Police Review Board

Film: "The Murder of Fred Hampton"

Panel & Speak Out:

Jeff Cohen
Co-chair Review Board Campaign

Anne Davis
Co-chair Review Board Campaign

Steve Durham
Freedom Socialist Party

Linda Lucas
Lesbians of Color

As targets for intensifying police crimes, lesbians, gay men, people of color and women have a vital stake in supporting the Campaign for a Citizens Police Review Board. Join us!

SATURDAY, FEB. 2, 7 p.m.

Door Donation: $2.00. All proceeds go to the Review Board Campaign

First Unitarian Church

Channing Hall, 2936 W. 8th Street (1 block east of Vermont) ·
Co-sponsored by: Campaign for a Citizens' Police Review Board and Lesbians of Color, Union of Lesbians and Gay Men, Black Panther Party, Feminist Women's Health Center, Lesbian and Gay Student Union (LACC), Radical Women and The Freedom Socialist Party.

Childcare available.   1/5/80
For information call 666-3217 or 463-3706   *Labor Donated*

FIGURE 2.5 Linda Lucas representing LOC at a Police Review Board Forum dated January 5, 1980. In "LOC LA" File, ONE Institute, Los Angeles.

dle, but I had a hard time holding it and keeping it lit. I finally discarded it, because I wanted to take in everything I was feeling and seeing, and I wanted my hands free so I could clap and pump my fists.

The section of Hollywood Boulevard we walked down was far from glamorous. That night, a few of the people accustomed to its street life and those whose livelihoods the march was interrupting gawked at us. I had to look twice at a group of sex workers standing on the sidewalk in front of the Snow White Café, pointing at us and calling us "crazy." And yet a few steps further down, some cheered us on. Independently owned restaurants and merchants, including some that sold-X rated materials, lined the street.

The city had not yet redeveloped the area into the mecca of Hollywood memorabilia it is now. It would take another decade of revitalization before a McDonald's restaurant considered opening up on this section of Hollywood Boulevard. Marilyn Monroe's star being added in 2016 certainly marked an effort to bring more attention to the area's transformation. Some might find the decision to locate it directly in front of the McDonald's entrance offensive, but it certainly attracts a different clientele than those who patronized the area in the 1980s.

Once we turned onto Highland, it did not take us long to reach the Mann's Hollywood Theatre, which was showing *Friday the 13th*. The procession slowed down, and loud "boos" and anger erupted because the film portrayed violence against women. A few steps further on the opposite side of the street stood a deep purple building with a pink awning over its front entrance: Fredrick's of Hollywood. Known for selling lingerie that hypersexualized and objectified women, it drew more boos and anger. The LOC contingent reacted angrily to these sites of women's exploitation too, but we also addressed another injustice. When we passed the police officers standing near barricades closing off the cross streets, some of us, mostly the African American women, got close to them and yelled in their faces, "No to Police Brutality!" and "Murderers!" multiple times. I had never witnessed such open declarations of emotion and hurt. I needed to step back and fight away tears as they seized the opportunity to voice the grievances they had to hold inside in their everyday lives. Although they were stoic, the police officers' expressions radiated revulsion.

I started to go with Renée to the Catch-One, or the Catch for short, on Saturday nights.[16] The owner, an African American woman named Jewel Thais-Williams, had established it in 1973. She was very hands on, always at the club smiling and welcoming patrons. It became an important place for me. Jewel and the Catch also played a critical role as a fundraising site in the 1980s, when HIV/AIDS exploded in the people-of-color community. One day in 1987, I showed up early to set up a voter registration table. Although I was allowed inside, Jewel asked me to be quiet, because a movie was being filmed. It turned out to be the major production *Beaches*. I stood in silence and observed as they filmed a scene on the dancefloor with Bette Midler and Barbara Hershey. Just like in the movies, when the director yelled "It's a wrap!" the cameras and everyone on set disappeared, and it became a typical throbbing Saturday night at the Catch again.

In 1979, many people from LOC also enjoyed the Catch. It was my initiation to dance clubs in Los Angeles, and it felt great to be part of the LOC group there. The Catch's pulsating, crowded dance floors and music surpassed my wildest fantasies. It had more than one large disco ball, and strobe lights changed colors and reflected off the people, mostly African American gay men, who filled the huge dance floor. The LOC group always started the night by dancing together, but people eventually broke off to dance with their partners, sit, or try to catch someone's eye.

Although I did not have great moves, I loved dancing. On my first night at the Catch, a gay man danced in front of me. We looked each other in the eye, smiled, and continued to move together until he wandered off. As I watched him, I realized he did not have a partner and was weaving through the dance floor dancing with those willing to move with him. He offered me an eye-opening and appealing option. While dancing with Renée, I wandered off and danced with the gay men next to us. A smile meant so many different things on the dance floor. In time, I traveled farther and felt a great sense of freedom. Each time I approached a new dancing partner, we flirted for a short time and then I moved on. No introductions, expectations, or commitments. I felt like I was floating.

I loved the autonomy and the sense of abandon I felt on the dance floor with men of color. Years later, at a white gay men's club, I encountered a few men who were having sex on the dancefloor. Although I got an eyeful, I became vigilant about not interrupting that activity and did not roam around as much. But it was all about dancing at the Catch. I played along when Black gay men backed their behind into me as we danced. On the rare occasions when men tried to front me, I instinctively moved away because it signaled that they were looking for something more. When I needed a break, water, or a sip of beer, I actively searched for Renée or the other LOC women.

Renée was lovely, but the fact that I worked at a mediocre job began to bother her. She did not understand why becoming an electrician was important to me, and she did not get it when I said, "I want to build things." Renée thought working in construction was beneath me and increasingly advised me to aspire toward a more professional career. We argued more often, and I began to distance myself from her, which meant avoiding the Catch for a while.

Timing is often everything. A new friend, Irene Martínez, popped into my life around this time, and we started going to Peanuts. The name remains a mystery, because it had nothing to do with Snoopy and the rest of Charles Schulz's characters. The building that once was Peanuts is now the Delilah, a trendy restaurant for hip celebrities located at 7969 Santa Monica Boulevard, in what is now West Hollywood. Before it became Peanuts, it was the Pink Pussycat and featured live nude shows. Even before I learned this, the top-to-bottom mirrored walls gave off a different vibe, which enhanced the disco feel.

Peanuts had a decent-sized dance floor. Irene and I often split up and looked for each other at closing time, when we would cross Santa Monica Boulevard to eat at Los Burritos in a strip mall. A little less than half of the people who went to Peanuts were Brown, and most were women. The crowd was in their early twenties. I often hung out with a few Latino guys on the dance floor, because asking a woman to dance seemed too stressful, and of course, they had the option of saying no. When I think of Peanuts, I think of Cheryl Lynn's "Got to Be Real," Diana Ross's "The Boss," Donna Summer, Sister Sledge, and of course "Funkytown."

When I started going to discos where women dominated the dance floor, like Peanuts and later Flamingo, the dynamics changed. I knew I could not wander through the dance floor, and I never tested the boundaries. Female couples dancing together were, for lack of a better word, territorial. When women danced together, they were making a public statement about their togetherness and being a couple. That was at the root of the fights that sometimes broke out between women at clubs.

Just looking at someone's partner could cause an eruption. I also never tried to get between women fighting on the dance floor; I moved out of the way. My friend Laura once tried to break up a fight; her white skirt ended up soaked in blood and she needed minor medical attention. A few times, gay men asked me, "Why do lesbians like to fight?" and shared that they were afraid of lesbians. I tried to explain why some women tried so hard to hold on to what they had. Finding love and a partner did not come easy, and some lesbians who felt threatened were willing to fight to maintain what they had.

The gay men at Peanuts, many of them Latinos, congregated in a corner of the dance floor away from the women. I danced and floated with them. It was this crowd that introduced me to poppers, or amyl nitrate, an inhalant that produced a brief high that got passed around the dance floor. I never asked how to ingest it, because all I needed to do was watch. It was an immediate high that lasted for only about a minute, but another small container would come around soon enough. When I sniffed poppers, I appreciated all the mirrors at Peanuts because I enjoyed watching myself dance in them.

A few times, some mod Chicanas came to the club. They were around my age, with spiky hairstyles and cool outfits. The four of them always danced together. Irene would come and get me when they arrived and say, "They're here." I would leave the dance floor and stand near the bar nursing a beer while staring at them. Attractive and hip, they often integrated punk moves into their dancing. I never thought of introducing myself, but once they arrived at Peanuts, they became my sole entertainment. This went on for a few months, until they showed up at a house party organized by someone in LOC. "You go to Peanuts," I said to them when we first met. They said yes, and one asked, "Do you go there?" I said sometimes, but I did not share that I stalked them at the club. I found out they were all born and raised in East Los Angeles. Finally, it seemed, my fantasy of hanging out with the Chicanas I ogled at Peanuts was close to coming true—but on this night, they were excited to share that they were leaving L.A. and moving to "the land."

I was floored to hear about their move. I had read about land women, but I thought that only white women who dressed down in plaid shirts and overalls moved to the land. I listened as they described why they found living with other women in a rural community so seductive. Most compelling to them was the opportunity to actively participate in building a new world with other women and to appreciate the bounty and beauty Mother Nature had to offer. It turned out that they had attended the Michigan Womyn's Music Festival and met a woman who invited them to Sassafras, women's land located in the Ozarks near Ponca, Arkansas. I got lost in the details, because I could not reconcile the fact that the women I considered the epitome of Brown L.A. cool were making a political decision to leave their life in L.A. behind them. I never saw them at Peanuts again, and Irene and I stopped going there a few months later because we both ended up in relationships. Peanuts closed around 1988.

From work to activism to the dance floor, my life evolved. I experienced a few different kinds of queer relationship patterns and learned what I wanted and what to steer clear of. I also became more comfortable exploring the joys of dancing with and learning about other queer peoples.

Looking back, I feel blessed to have been a part of LOC in 1979 and the early 1980s. At that time, we did not have mentors to emulate or that could offer us advice. Queer radical feminist writers of color such as Audre Lorde had not yet written about the tools needed to dismantle the master's house, and notable works such as *This Bridge Called My Back: Writings by Radical Women of Color*, a feminist anthology edited by Cherríe Moraga and Gloria E. Anzaldúa, had not yet been published. Clearly, many of the conversations and actions that those active in LOC engaged in were groundbreaking. It is striking that all the queer bars and discos I mentioned in this chapter have closed, and now exist only in memory. Even LOC stopped meeting in the mid-1980s. Yet the issues of homophobia, violence against women and queers, racism, and police brutality remain salient and potent.

CHAPTER 3

When Forward was the Only Option

A t its core, identity is about connecting. I knew I was queer the moment my consciousness had evolved enough to formulate thoughts. As I ventured further out in the world as a child, the racism and exclusion I experienced made me realize that I was also Brown. In 1969, when I learned about the Chicano Movement in junior high school, I instantly connected with it and self-identified as a Chicana. This identity made me feel that I belonged to a group that shared similar cultural and historical experiences of growing up in the U.S. Equally important, asserting "I am a Chicana" made me feel like I participated in a movement that empowered me to speak out against injustice and to be a political person out in the world. My involvement in Lesbians of Color gave me the opportunity to have meaningful discussions about race and solidarity with people of color, and I recognized that we were at the vanguard, carving out a space for ourselves and building new networks and communities. I knew white gays and lesbians had organized a movement, but I never felt part of it.

I never considered myself rebellious. Instead, when I think back, I see a person seeking to belong in spaces where I felt empowered. As a Chicana in the late 1970s and 1980s, I encountered a queer scene where I could assert, "I am a Chicana," but where there was little room for gender ambiguity. Lesbian social circles and codes at the time did not require that I behave or dress like a woman, but I often felt pressured to embrace being one. In late 1979, I helped relaunch a group called Lesbianas Latina Americanas, or La Las. A few people in the group enjoyed referring to those around them as diosas, or goddesses. I bristled the few times they referred to me as diosa, and when I asked them not to, one retorted, "Who wouldn't want to be called a diosa?"

Back then I had no inkling why I did not want others to attach certain words and labels to me. I know now that I felt uncomfortable identifying as a woman. This deep-seated feeling, which was far from an awareness, prevented me from embracing a lesbian identity. Instead of saying, "I am a lesbian," I mostly referred myself as a dyke. To me, the term *dyke* seemed more to the point, and it reflected my masculine-leaning resourcefulness: I could change a tire and tinker under the hood of my car, and I could not wait to be part of a construction crew. Despite my lingering discomfort, lesbian spaces came closest to mirroring my experiences and desires at that time. I also felt a strong sense of belonging in lesbian of color spaces and groups. I shied away from identifying as butch, because I did not feel like I was playing a role.[1] I identify as nonbinary now, but even that category is starting to seem too broad, and I am feeling the need for something different.

We were also less inclined to use the term *identity* in the late 1970s and 1980s to associate ourselves with political behaviors or categories related to pride, ethnicity, or race, as we do today. We had to wait another decade to say "I identify as_____." We did not use the word gender, and we were stuck in a binary where people were either men or women. We did not have the words or language to discuss what people like me were feeling. Back then, the overarching assumption was that every woman who sought the company of and sexually desired women was a lesbian. Lesbians that identified as butch were considered masculine women. It is not that we did not talk about gender during my early days in L.A.—we discussed it excessively. We just did not refer to it as gender. In fact, soon after I arrived in Los Angeles, in 1979, a *Tide* cover story dove into this issue. The nuances of gender today were far off. At the time, lesbian was an undisputed category, and within that grouping, women identified themselves and others as playing feminine- or masculine-leaning roles.

The *Tide* asked, "Are Roles Really Dead?" It offered insights from a Butch/Femme survey and interviews they had conducted of a cross-section of lesbians. The *Tide* divided the respondents into two main groups: old-gay (women that the *Tide* determined were not feminist) and radical lesbian feminists. Those who did not fit into either category were referred to as "mixed." In her "To Role or Not to Role" assessment, publisher and writer Jeanne Cordova, along with other contributors from the *Tide*, initially and insightfully alluded to the limitations imposed by language. "Some polarizing opinion about role playing may be fueled more by a language barrier," she wrote. Cordova and the *Tide* also determined that the survey illuminated "one commonality" among all the respondents: how peer and societal pressures weighed heavily on a group in which fixed gender identities prevailed. The *Tide* reported that their respondents "blamed others for what roles they did have. Straight society, the 'gay world,' and the feminist community were alternately at fault."[2]

It should be noted that Cordova and the *Tide* took on this survey in a time when social scientists did not find lesbian relationships worthy of study. Queer Studies remained decades away, and the nuances of gender and its fluidity were beyond discussion. As language regarding gender and identities evolved and became more expansive, so did our gender affiliations. No longer content to "blame" others for assigning us categories, queers would create new ones and claim them.

Interestingly, Cordova cited Shirl Buss's response in the survey. She had been a writer for the *Tide*. "I go in and out of both roles," she said. "In my work (carpenter) I'm into my butch side, at home the way I joke and play is more what I'd call swishy femme."[3] I met Shirl after some relationship detours, a year after that survey appeared in print, and she would become an important part of my life. Around that time, in 1982, I also became part of the electrical union Local 11 in Los Angeles, which would help me cultivate another aspect of my identity as an electrician in the construction trades.

At this time in my life, I did most of my shopping at stores in Alhambra's adjoining city of Monterey Park, which were all less than a five-minute drive from my apartment. I bought groceries at the Alpha Beta Supermarket, and I purchased bedding, a clothes hamper and kitchen items at the PicNSave. I also found my go-to Mexican food place, Manny's El Loco. I had never seen such a wide selection of burritos, and their Chile Relleno became my favorite. When I told my mother, she remarked, "Who would put a Chile Relleno inside a burrito?" Great demographic changes were happening in Alhambra and Monterey Park. Asian immigrants were buying homes and establishing businesses. Strip malls popped up to cater to consumer needs, with optometrists, medical clinics, seafood restaurants, and new banks, all with Mandarin names.

I had a keen eye for observing changes in my surroundings. As a child in Tucson during the 1960s, I witnessed the undoing of a neighborhood of Brown people who started moving out, one family at a time. I also observed how the white power structure used their power to further the image of my hometown as an "American" city. Those in high places used urban renewal to destroy close to 80 acres, removing largely Mexican and Mexican American people and destroying numerous older Sonoran Row Houses. The "renewal" part, grounded in racist notions of making Tucson appear more "American" and therefore more white, meant replacing Mexican people with a new concrete civic and convention center.[4]

A different type of urban renewal was taking place in Alhambra and Monterey Park. Buildings were not leveled, but assigned a different purpose. The influx of Asians and Asian Americans was revitalizing a mundane white suburban landscape. Collectively, the new residents and business owners transformed sites to serve their consumer and cultural needs. Heeding rules grounded in capitalist notions of landownership, Asian and Asian American investors started buying up properties. White developers and building owners profited from selling their properties to them at inflated prices. The PicNSave I once shopped at became a Big Lots and then a Superco 皇都電器 that sold furniture and mattresses. Alpha Beta became the Shun Fat Supermarket, and El Loco was one of the handful of Mexican American businesses that eventually disappeared.[5]

I coveted how Asian and Asian American people moved through their spaces and spoke their language freely in Monterey Park and Alhambra. It was enthralling to see these new arrivals who felt entitled to embrace their culture in public spaces. Sure, I had observed Mexicans and Mexican Americans freely speaking Spanish on the streets in Boyle Heights as a child and in the late 1970s, but they did not own the majority of the establishments. Menus and commercial signage were not yet in Spanish. The McDonald's on Soto Street and East César E. Chávez Avenue in Boyle Heights would never have been welcomed in the heart of Monterey Park.

The changes I witnessed in Monterey Park and Alhambra made me reflect on the burden that people of color from my parent's generation had placed on themselves to assimilate, or at least to appear assimilated. I recalled riding the bus once with my mother, Chita, when I was around ten. Chita typically spoke to me in Spanish, but on the bus that day, she kept speaking to me rather loudly in English. When we got off the bus, I asked her why, and she said, "I want gringos to see and hear that we know how to speak English." Her efforts to impress whites troubled me, even at that young age. What I witnessed in Alhambra and Monterey Park, twenty years after that bus ride, was Asian and Asian American cultural pride and visibility. The people who moved, shopped, and established businesses there were not trying to impress white people.

The accommodation of the ethnic and racial changes in Alhambra was not all encompassing, unfortunately: my landlord had a problem with queers converging on his property. Using my small second-story apartment as meeting headquarters for Latina lesbians in 1979 came with a price. A few—eight at the most—gathered in my apartment to connect with others like them. The onsite manager, whose father owned the building, made a point of talking to me one day as I entered my apartment. "Who are all these women coming over to your apartment on Saturday evenings?" she asked. "Friends," I replied. "I don't think my father would approve." My gut reaction was to retort, "I am sure he would not," but I remained silent. As I walked up the stairs, the question, "Do they think I am hosting an orgy?" crossed my mind, but they might have considered the reality of Latina lesbians organizing on their property equally distasteful. My landlord's concerns were more than mere warnings, though. About two weeks later, he started implementing a series of rent increases.

Renée and some others often told me about another Chicana, Irene, who had not been around the Lesbians of Color group in a while, but whom

I needed to meet. In a city as big as Los Angeles, that only a single Chicana had made an impression on the women in LOC concerned me. A few also asked if I had met Yolanda. I said, "I don't think so?" and was told, "Well, if you did you would remember." I finally met both in early September of 1979.

As soon as she walked into a LOC meeting, I knew she was the infamous Yolanda Retter. Renée confirmed this, pointing her chin toward her. During the meeting, I read her demeanor as dismissive, because she did not address the group and she directed her comments mainly toward Ntianu, who often seemed to run the group. After the meeting, however, Yolanda made a beeline toward me. We both had longish hair and wore jeans and a tee shirt, but her clothes were much baggier than mine. Yolanda had a biethnic and binational background. She been born in New Haven, Connecticut to a Peruvian mother and white US American father with a degree from Harvard, but she had spent most of her childhood in El Salvador.[6] She was eight years older than me.

She did not bother to introduce herself, but in a strange way seemed to read my mind. "You want to meet more Latinas, don't you?" she asked. I had been disappointed that I had not met a single Chicana in the month I started attending LOC, but I tried not to act surprised by how accurately she read me. I simply nodded. Yolanda's next question caught me by surprise, too. "Do you have your own place?" Again, I just nodded. "Good" she said, "I'll call a group of Latinas and we'll meet at your house on Saturday." I thought the request was unusual, coming from someone I just met, but I said, "Sure" and gave Yolanda my phone number and address.

Although I doubted the meeting would happen, I began to feel self-conscious that week, because although I had furniture, my apartment looked a bit barren. Yolanda called around noon on Wednesday, before I left for work. She cut right to the chase and stated, "The meeting is on. We'll be at your house at 6:00 on Saturday." I skipped the movies that day to straighten up my apartment.

Eventually, Yolanda, Irene Martínez, and María Dolores Díaz knocked on my door. María had been born and raised in Honduras and had a PhD. Maya, who was extremely quiet and never affiliated herself with a nationality, also attended. At twenty-four, I was the youngest in the group; Irene was approaching thirty, and María and Maya were around forty.

Yolanda had invited Irene and Maya to the meeting, but they did not seem close. Yolanda and María, however, were good friends. Both had college degrees, were from privileged backgrounds, and grew up in Latin America. They often broke away and spoke to each other in Spanish. I understood what they were saying, but Irene and Maya did not. The group dynamic felt off, but I remembered that my first LOC meeting had not gone so well either. I had expected to feel much more connected with Latinas, though. At the first meeting, Yolanda and María spent most of the time recounting all the Latinas they had met in other white lesbian events and groups. We decided to meet the next Saturday at my apartment again, even though I had only provided potato chips and tap water. It was clear that since we had found each other, the next step was to form a group. Maya never returned to the group, however, although I saw her at other events in the future.

Irene was the first out Chicana I met in Los Angeles, and we bonded immediately. She was born and raised in Los Angeles, moving often as a child until her parents bought a house in Azuza, close to thirty miles northeast of Los Angeles. Her family was working class, and she never attended college. She stayed after the meeting and we talked until sunup. I asked Irene how she had learned about LOC. She was not sure, but deduced it could have been on the radio or through a posting on a bulletin board at Sojourner, a women's bookstore in Long Beach, where she lived at the time. She recalled that a small index card that read "LOC, LOC, LOC" in big letters caught her attention, but she might have heard about LOC on IMRU, a queer radio collective radio on KPFK or 90.7 FM, which had started broadcasting "Lesbian Sisters" bimonthly in 1978.

Marylyn Rodriguez joined us at the next meeting. She was a gregarious Chicana who spoke Spanish well and had known Yolanda and Maria for a while. She was the first woman I met who openly identified as a lipstick lesbian. In many ways, she helped bridge the gap between the Chicanas and the other two Latinas, because she was very touchy with everyone. She actually pulled us physically together before and after the meetings. When Yolanda and María started talking about white lesbians or groups we did not know, Marylyn would say to them, "Explain who they are."

Yolanda suggested we name ourselves Lesbianas Latina Americanas. She said it had been used by a group that no longer met and that they called themselves La Las for short. Yolanda never shared much about the group or why neither she nor María had been a part of it. The original La Las group that met in 1974 remained a mystery to me until I started writing this book. It turns out someone I knew, Estilita Grimaldo, had helped start the original group. When we met in the early 1980s, she owned a travel agency called WomanTours, and we sometimes bumped into each other at social events. She also helped me with travel reservations, but she never shared details about her efforts to organize Latina lesbians. Of course, I am guilty of never asking.[7]

That evening, María looked into my bedroom as the group headed to the door, where I had taped up some photographs I had cut out from magazines. One of them caught María's attention: a black-and-white photograph of Felix Unger and Oscar Madison, the main characters of the sitcom *The Odd Couple*. It had aired in the early to mid 1970s, but I often watched it in reruns. Through my queer lens, I considered Oscar and Felix as portraying closeted gay characters. They were the adult version of Ernie and Bert on *Sesame Street*. I was not alone in these impressions—I once tried to convince my mother to watch *The Odd Couple* with me, and she said, "Is that show with the two jotos?" It was my first direct experience with lesbian separatism, and women who arranged their lives so they had little contact with men, gay or straight. María loudly demanded of me, "Take this down!" "It's Oscar and Felix," I timidly retorted. "Yes," she said with much authority, "I know, but you don't want men or even pictures of men in your apartment." I was thrown off. "I don't."

Yolanda, who had walked out the door, heard María and returned to loudly confirm, "No. You don't!" I remained silent as they both walked out and down the stairs, stunned by what had just happened in my own house. I put the issue aside and sat down with Irene on the couch, but before the next La Las meeting, I relented and removed the photograph.

I resented it, though. At the next meeting, Yolanda and María noted that I had taken down the photo and related their approval—not to me, but to each other.

I certainly recognized the oppressive patriarchal system we lived in and recognized male privilege. I knew how pervasive a system it is, but growing up, I had also witnessed women promoting patriarchal ideals. They elevated men and condoned submissive roles for women. I also had felt close to some of the men in my family, and I had close male friends in high school. I would come to learn that most of the women I organized with—and I include myself in this assessment—were lesbian separatists to varying degrees, but most were not as extreme as Yolanda and María. I respected it, and I was protective about ensuring lesbians of color had our own spaces where we could discuss and share issues.

La Las often discussed needing to spread the word so other Latina lesbians would eventually join our group. I took charge of planning a dance a few months later, in the hopes of making a statement about our existence, and that of La Las. Not many dance halls allowed us to hold queer events, but LOC had held events at the Church at Ocean Park in Santa Monica. The next week, I placed a call to Judy Abdo, who operated the church, and made an appointment to meet with her.

The Catholic priests and nuns I had known back home would never have allowed queers to use their facilities. When I arrived and looked up at the Church in Ocean Park, it looked like a church I had seen in films, and I thought, "This is the type of church Dorothy from the 'Wizard of Oz' attended when she lived in Kansas." Once inside, I took a long look at the stained-glass windows depicting Jesus in different settings. They were colorful and beautiful, and they reminded me of the ones at the Santa Cruz Church back in Tucson. When we reached the large second-floor meeting space with the decorative light fixtures, I knew instantly that the wooden floors would make an excellent dance floor. We scheduled our event for June 7, 1980. Although Abdo expected a deposit, she generously made an exception for La Las. "You can pay us after the event," she said. I could not wait to call Irene to tell her and to start working on the flyer and plan for the dance. We started by posting flyers at bars and bookstores all over.

In the latter part of September of 1979, Emma Pérez started showing up at LOC meetings with her African American partner, Cheryl. Yolanda had invited Emma, a Chicana enrolled in a master's program in History at UCLA, to also attend the La Las meetings. She brought new energy to the group, and it became apparent that Yolanda respected her knowledge of Marxist and feminist theory. Because we prioritized building bridges with the Brown community, Emma and I and the other Chicanas, Irene and Marylyn, started meeting more frequently outside of La Las. We also liked to go out dancing as a group.

Someone brought up that the La Raza Student Coalition was holding a "Día de La Mujer" Conference at California State University at Long Beach. It was the winter of 1979, and all of us had experienced the homophobia in Chicano and Chicana activists' spaces and communities that used terms like *sisterhood* or *hermandad* to describe Chicana unity. We decided to test how inclusive they really were.

Once in Long Beach, we walked into an open area, registered, and sat through some workshops. Between sessions, a woman playing a guitar strolled around singing Chicano movement and protest songs, like "De Colores" and "We Shall Not Be Moved." We were a fun and lively group, and we sang along. Some of the more mature women were taken by our youthful energy. I could tell that they appreciated us and considered us the next generation of emerging Chicana activists—which we were, but we were also queer!

The Coalition gathered in the courtyard for a large session in the afternoon. I noticed Emma and Marylyn strategizing with each other before we sat at a table together. When Emma sensed the session was coming to an end, she whispered something to Marylyn, stood up, and walked over to the woman holding the microphone. She had a brief conversation with her, and the woman said, "Hermanas, we have an important announcement." I was surprised that it happened so swiftly. Marylyn immediately stood up to address the crowd. She said something like, "Estamos aquí en solidaridad con todos ustedes en Día de la Mujer. Somos tus hermanas pero también somos lesbianas. Nuestras familias y comunidades se nie-

We as Latina Lesbians encourage the Latino/Latina community
to acknowledge our struggle for human rights in this society
that oppress all minority people. We voice this statement
today so that we can begin to dispel the negative stereotypes
in our Latino/Latina Community. For centuries we have been
vitimized by a society that has catogorized us as diviant
and perverse. We know that we fit neither of these catogories.
We know that we are your sisters, tia's, and friends.

FIGURE 3.1 Handouts distributed by Lesbianas Latina Americanas at the "Dia de La Mujer" Conference. Private collection of Irene Martínez and Laura Duran.

gan a reconocer que existimos, pero estamos aquí y estamos orgullosas."
(We are here in solidarity with all of you. We are your sisters but we are also lesbians. Our families and communities refuse to acknowledge that we exist but we are here and we are proud.) By this point, her voice started to waiver with emotion. I too underestimated the intense feelings that flooded into my body. We passed out the flyers we had prepared stating our position as lesbians in the community.

All eyes were on us. What had once been loving glances turned hostile. The women seated at our table scurried away immediately so they would not be associated with us. The woman with the guitar disappeared. I remember turning to observe the faces of the women who moved away but who continued to gawk at us. Most were shocked, but I also saw confusion on many of their faces. After a few minutes, a woman approached us and sternly said, "You better leave!" I cannot confirm if she was with the La Raza Student Coalition or a representative, but we obliged. We exited slowly. No one attempted to intervene on our behalf. Once outside the building, we high-fived and congratulated each other, but we listened to the radio and self-reflected on the drive home.

The La Las dance in March went off seamlessly and was well attended. Yolanda collected the money at the door. Other than Marylyn, people did not dance much to the salsa music we offered. It had not yet exploded in popularity, although a few years earlier the *L.A. Times* wrote that Chicanos and Chicanas were taking to the dancefloor "not to do the disco duck or hustle or any current 'get-up-and-boogie crazes.' These kids were doing their own Latin thing [to] . . . a beat they call salsa."[8] Most of the lesbians at the dance preferred to mingle, and not many Latinas attended the event. Those who did were with white partners. A few African American women from LOC attended, and a lot of white women showed up to support our new group. We made money at the door and raised enough to pay for the hall rental.

The highlight of the evening was when Emma introduced me to Shirl Buss. I remember that we shook hands and she looked me in the eye and smiled. Her girlfriend, who acted rather serious, stood next to her. In fact, everyone at the dance seemed to be in a couple. I saw Shirl again the next month, when Emma and Cheryl held a party at their small apartment in Santa Monica. She was standing near the food table, and she smiled at me across the room. I walked towards her to say hello. We were about the same height, although she was a bit slighter in build and was white.

Shirl was generous with her smiles and, as I would later learn, generous about all things that mattered in the world. We talked, laughed, and even danced, but it was hard because the apartment was so small and crowded. When I asked about her girlfriend, she said, "We broke up." I liked the response, but I did not think I had a chance with Shirl. She left early and I stayed behind. When I walked to my car, I saw what looked like a parking ticket on the windshield. It was a note from Shirl asking that I call her. I considered it a charming gesture, but my life felt too complicated at that point. Although Emma and Cheryl were still a couple, Emma and I had formed an attraction to each other through our work in La Las and LOC.

Even though the La Las group remained few in number, some in LOC were starting to resent that the Latinas were meeting separately. Irene, Emma, and I continued to attend LOC meetings, but holding the dance and raising our own separate funds concerned some of the LOC members. They were afraid not so much that we were breaking away, but that we were having our cake and eating it too. Matu and Morena, who moved to L.A. from the Bay Area, picked up on the tensions. Matu was Puerto Rican and played guitar and drums. Morena was an African American with an interest in photography. They both worked in the construction trades. The couple appreciated LOC's potential to organize politically, and also to build relationships across ethnic and racial lines. Along with Emma, they spearheaded a series of workshops, or rap groups, as they

Rap Group Topics

April 20   Self Hate
May 4   What is support? Building a system within
            Lesbians of Color
May 18   Self-Help presentation
June 1   Feminism
June 15   Demonstrations, laws. and legislation
June 29   Work: Dealing with sexism and racism on the job
July 13   Child Abuse, unwanted pregnancy
July 27   Bisexuals, Lesbians, and separatists
August 10   Monogamy and. nonmonogamy

Topics can be changed depending on the situation at the time. If
a sister comes in needing to deal with something else than what
is scheduled, her need should be considered by the whole group
or concerned individuals. If an instance of racism in the community
needs to be confronted with the support of the whole group, we
will take our time to deal with that first.

FIGURE 3.2 Rap group flyer from 1980. Private collection of Irene Martínez and
Laura Duran.

were called at the time. They asked that we come to the sessions with
open hearts and minds. We discussed many issues, such as internalized
racism, homophobia and interethnic differences, which Morena called
horizontal hostility.

Most LOC members appreciated Matu and Morena's dedication to
our collective and individual wellbeing and political growth. They were
a bit older, and the love and sensitivity with which they conducted the
sessions made everyone feel welcomed and connected. I waited in an-
ticipation for these gatherings; so did everyone else, because attendance
at the rap groups was much higher than for ordinary LOC meetings.
After the workshops, they held parties at their house and encouraged
us to continue our conversations. They were great teachers. Instead of
works by white feminists, they suggested reading the Combahee River
Collective's statement to further appreciate the power of Black feminism
and to locate ourselves in the multiple and overlapping systems of "racial, sexual, heterosexual, and class oppression" that we now refer to as
intersectionality.[9]

FIGURE 3.3 Group Photograph of LOC taken on the porch of Matu and Morena's house after a rap session, 1980. Private collection of author.

Matu and Morena also organized camping trips for us. Once, when we checked into a National Forest campground, the ranger asked us what LOC stood for. I was behind the steering wheel and caught off guard when an African American woman in the back seat yelled out, "Lovers of Camping." We all broke out laughing. A look of skepticism crossed the ranger's face, but he let us enter the campground. Unfortunately, a year later, Matu and Morena moved on, because they could not find a way to break into the unionized construction trades. To me, it seemed that energy in LOC slowly dissipated after they left.

By the end of the summer of 1980, Emma had broken up with Cheryl. My Alhambra apartment had become a sort of clubhouse, and a few times I allowed women to stay there when they needed. Emma took it a step further and moved in. She had no furniture, just a few boxes. We enjoyed all that we had in common. Both of us had moved to L.A. to embrace our Brown and queer selves—me from Arizona and she from Texas, where we were each raised. At the same time, we were very different. We never talked about our future together or discussed household finances, but for a brief time, we were a couple.

By then, the end of La Las seemed imminent. Yolanda and María Dolores often insisted that we use the group as a platform to "Call out white women on their bullshit," but that was the last thing the Chicanas wanted to invest their energies in. Romantic liaisons, including my relationship with Emma, were causing tensions, and the group had lost steam. Emma and I ended breaking up in the early months of 1981, and the tensions in La Las had caused my arms and upper body to erupt in itchy red spots. Despite a number of consultations with dermatologists, the rash would not go away. When the group ended, La Las entrusted the funds we had raised to Ntianu, who took care of the LOC finances for safekeeping, but we made a pact with her that La Las would decide where the funds should be allocated in the future.

I had kept Shirl's number, and we set up a time to meet for lunch. Because Shirl was a carpenter, she was excited to learn that I too wanted to learn a skill and enter the trades. Shirl was also a licensed contractor who had cofounded an all-women construction company called Building Women. Her accomplishments, in addition to her attractiveness and energy, blew me away. There seemed to not be enough hours in a day for us. To say our humor clicked is an understatement, because we laughed all the time. Maybe this is why the rashes on my body started to slowly disappear. Throughout our relationship, I often complained because Shirl frequently asked me deep or "meaning of life" questions, but at the same time, I appreciated that she was interested in knowing my thoughts and feelings. It was nice to feel loved and to count on someone to always be there for me.

It also helped that Shirl was six years older than me. I recognized that her white privilege had allowed her more educational opportunities than most of the other women I had met in Los Angeles, but I also appreciated that she knew more than I did about everything I wanted to know more about. She did not want to change me, and she was invested in helping me grow as person. The fact that she knew everyone and everything added to her allure. After all, she was Shirl Buss, whom I had gotten to know over the years as a writer for the *Tide*! I was smitten.

Shirl and I spent our first nights together at my Alhambra apartment but quickly ended up moving in together. We fit the stereotype associated with the popular joke, "What does a lesbian bring on a second date? A U-Haul." Our decision was prompted by my frequent rent increases, and because Shirl and I sincerely wanted to spend more time with each other. After a month, we packed up my belongings and I moved in with her. She and her former partner had purchased a home in Venice, and Shirl had used her carpentry skills to transform the garage that sat in the back. A huge yard full of lush plants and even a koi pond separated the two houses. When my mother came to visit, she said the yard felt like a garden paradise. The sounds of birds outside also reminded me of the time I spent in Boyle Heights with my tía Mincy.

The former double garage behind the main house, which we would now call an accessory unit, was wisely designed, and Shirl had dedicated every inch to a precise purpose. Although she never imagined that two people would one day live there, I fit in seamlessly, as I did not have many belongings. No boxes ever cluttered the small kitchen or living room. Shirl even managed to have a drafting table near the window. Double

FIGURE 3.4 Shirl Buss and author in 1981. Private collection of author.

doors opened up to the garden, which made the space feel boundless, and the upstairs loft served as the bedroom.

Venice was in the midst of becoming more upscale in the early 1980s. Our small cottage had a wood-burning stove, and I became an expert at using an axe to split wood. In the years I lived there, there was an abundance of construction projects in the area. The sites were dormant on weekends, and we would cruise around job sites in Shirl's red diesel Volkswagen truck and pick up scrap pieces of 2×4s or 2×6s and use them to heat our house.

Building Women encouraged women to enter the construction trades. They provided classes that taught women basic skills and repairs and let them know that working in the trades was a career option. As a small business, Building Women prioritized serving low-income residents and aimed to get involved in a project that provided low-cost housing for women and children. I did not have many skills and tried to shadow Shirl everywhere. I occasionally helped out, mostly on weekends.

Those years provided respite for me, and I loved living in Venice. I no longer had to worry about making large rent payments, and I started putting money aside. I quit my job as a proofer when a Local 11 agent contacted me and told me to expect to be called upon to work in three months. I prioritized getting fit and started jogging five miles a day. Building Women had a contract with the City of Santa Monica to install deadbolt and window locks for those with limited incomes. Shirl showed me how to install the devices and threw a few assignments my way to provide me some extra income.

Shirl and I had great times. Her love for the L.A. Dodgers was contagious, and the team rallied from behind to win a World Series in 1981. I came to appreciate announcer Vin Scully's enthusiasm, and attending games at Dodger Stadium blew me away. Shirl knew the westside of L.A. well, and she often pointed out celebrity's houses when we drove around, like where Marilyn Monroe lived and died. In 1982, we went to see Prince perform at the Santa Monica Civic Center for my birthday. We also participated in a number of political marches against U.S. intervention in Central America and against violence against women. We joined a few United Farm Worker (UFW) protests against supermarkets that bought

FIGURE 3.5 Author at home in Venice in 1982. Private collection of author.

lettuce from boycotted growers, and we once walked behind the UFW banner in a long march led by César Chávez from Santa Monica to Pacific Palisades. I rushed up to the front often to talk to him and made mundane comments such as "You know we're here for you, César." He was very responsive but I would get intimidated and fall back to walk with Shirl for a while. Soon after, I would muster up the courage and rush to the front to talk to him again. Chávez would smile each time he saw me, and it was exhausting for me.

Shirl and I valued our independence, and each of us had a separate circle of friends. I continued to hang out with Irene, although I did not go to clubs that often. I also attended LOC meetings and functions. I volunteered to help with the Halloween Dance, and took care of many of the arrangements. I chuckle at my lack of creativity regarding the costume I wore—a lavender ghost. The event was well attended, and seeing so many women in costumes was unforgettable.

I spent most Sundays at the Venice boardwalk milling around, people watching, and enjoying pizza, cokes, and ice cream. Many people converged there on Sundays, as they still do, but in the early 1980s Venice

FIGURE 3.6 Anna (left) and Marylyn (right) at the Halloween Dance, 1980. Private collection of author.

had more of a hippie vibe. The sidewalk vending was more makeshift—
vendors would just set up a table. Roller skating was in fashion, and the
dare-devil performances, such as jumping over huge obstacles on skates,
eating fire, and walking on glass, were astonishing. I could not help but
try out new sunglasses each time I visited. I sometimes met friends at
the boardwalk, but mostly I enjoyed spending Sundays by myself, people
watching and enjoying the ocean.

Shirl sometimes came with me to the boardwalk, but she often had to go over plans or organize materials for the coming week. I witnessed the intense energy she invested into Building Women. She woke up early to be at the lumber yard, to ensure her various job sites had the necessary materials, and she often worked late and on weekends. Taking care of the business side of Building Women was hard work, too. Although I greatly admired Shirl's efforts, it confirmed for me that I wanted a job like my tío Mando's. He came home after working hard and did not need to worry about clients, lining up the next project, contacts that fell through, or if checks bounced.

I was living in Venice when I received the call from Local 11 to be part of the cohort of new apprentices. The local was divided into subdistricts according to address, and I was assigned to District (or Dispatch) 3. This encompassed the beach communities, West Los Angeles, and the airport. For the next four years, in addition to working 40 hours, I attended mandatory classes two nights a week in a large rectangular room with the brightest florescent lights in town. There were repercussions to missing classes, and I did not miss many. Typically, I went home after work, cleaned up, ate an early dinner, and would arrive in time for my class in a building Local 11 owned near the airport. We were reminded often that we would need to pass an extensive exam to become journeyman linemen at the end of our four-year apprenticeships.

To say I was nervous in the days leading up to my first job is an understatement. I had attended some pre-apprenticeship classes and had received instructions to buy a tool pouch and belt, as well as a list of hand tools I needed to purchase and bring with me on my first day of work. Shirl went with me to purchase them. In terms of my wardrobe, my mother was visiting from Tucson and accompanied me while I shopped for new jeans. She was 69 years old, and after dedicating so much of her energy to making me wear dresses and act like "a girl" when I was growing up, she recognized how this new work adventure and wardrobe best fit my interests. When we reached the cashier, Chita volunteered to pay for my two pairs of jeans. On the way back to the car, she chuckled, "You finally found a job where you can wear these to work! Aye Lydia." I put my arm around her and we laughed together.

On July 26, 1982, I was dispatched to the Howard Hughes Corporate Headquarters in the Westchester district of Los Angeles.[10] It had taken me almost two years to get to this point. The outside walls were completed, and the job site was spread out. My dispatch sheet instructed me to look for the trailer with the electrical company's name, AMELCO, on it. It also said to ask for Slim, the on-site supervisor. I parked my car where it seemed that everyone else did, carried my tool belt around my shoulder and a sandwich Shirl had made me stuffed into a brown paper bag, and walked into the trailer. The two guys inside looking at blueprints turned to look at me. I looked at the tall thin one, said, "Are you Slim?" and held out my dispatch sheet. "So you're who the local sent," he said. He looked me over and told me, "I want you to know that I don't want you here but I have to take you because the local sent you." In all the conversations I had with electricians' union representatives, they had given me the impression that women had already been integrated and welcome. I was not expecting to be a trailblazer. So much raced through my head at that moment, but I remained silent, looked Slim in the eye, and awaited his next move.

Slim put his hard hat on, reached into a box and handed me a new hardhat, and said, "Put this on." I followed him out of the trailer, wearing a hard hat for the first time in my life.

I remember looking back and catching a glimpse of the ocean in the distance. Even though Slim did not approve of me, I felt impressed with myself for simply being on such a large-scale construction project. Thinking this helped me shake off the anxiety. Once we entered the building, I noted that all the workers were male, and only a few were Brown. None looked surprised to see me or said anything, but they noticed me. When we found the general foreman, Slim finally looked at my dispatch statement to find my name. "This is Lydia," he said. "Put her to work." I watched him walk away, and a curse word crossed my mind, but not my lips.

The foreman was much nicer than Slim. He walked me over to Charlie Rogers, the first journeyman I would work under out of about thirty during my four apprentice years. I say "under" because the electrical union was structured to ensure that apprentices knew their place and respected journeymen. Union protocols prohibited apprentices from working independently. It was assumed that we should be supervised by a qualified and learned electrician, who would watch out for our safety and share their knowledge with us.

Charlie was a traveler—someone who belonged to another IBEW local but got an opportunity to work in L.A. because additional labor was needed. He lived in a recreational vehicle with four other guys, because he did not want to settle down in Los Angeles, and he knew that travelers were the first laid off when a project neared completion. The good news was that Charlie was from Arizona, and we bonded immediately. He had worked as an electrician at the Palo Verde Nuclear Generating Station and lived in Phoenix. Between talking about nuclear energy and how the reactors produced electricity, Charlie showed me where to retrieve long pieces of metal channel and how to cut them into the two-foot pieces we need to build supports that held the electrical conduit routed through the ceiling. He also showed me where the goggles were kept, and warned me to always to wear them.

The orderly construction site impressed me, as did the fact that my hard hat, the googles, and the machinery I was using were all new. Charlie also found me a new pair of gloves and showed me where the portable water dispensers for electricians were—each trade had their own—and where the portable bathrooms were outside. Typically, one was reserved for the women on the job sites. I was the only tradesperson, but some administrative assistants who worked in the company trailers used them as well.

I took great care to measure correctly, and Charlie instructed me not to rush. He emphasized that I needed to learn to do everything correctly. Some other electricians stopped by and introduced themselves. We never shook hands, but each asked what year I was in the apprentice program. When I said it was my first day, all of them said, "You're just a cub!" which appealed to me, because it seemed endearing and everything seemed new and bewildering to me. I learned later that electricians traditionally refer to first-year apprentices as cubs.

I observed how each of the different construction trades claimed a separate work area. Electricians never ate lunch or spent their breaks with those from the other trades. When we performed our jobs, we sometimes talked to painters, drywallers, or other tradespeople, but electricians made a point of sticking together. The gang boxes imprinted with the electrical company's name—the large metal storage containers where we secured the company's and our own personal tools when we had finished for the day—became our designated area. At lunchtime on my first day, Charlie told me, "We all eat over here." He walked me to "our" area, and I sat on the floor to eat my sandwich with the electricians. Except for one African American man, all of them were white. After my interaction with Slim, I was surprised to find them welcoming. A few shared how intimidated they had been on the first day of their apprentice program, which I appreciated.

When the workday ended around 3:30 pm, all the electricians gathered around the gang box to drop off their tools. Some talked about their day and reminded the foreman they were running short of certain conduit or supplies. I put my tools in the gang box too, because I was part of a team and was coming back the next day. As I reflect back, I really do not know how I made it, except that I wanted it so intensely. Shirl was waiting for me when I got home. In recounting my day, it seemed like two separate events: my encounter with Slim, which was terrible, and a spectacular day where I learned and got to do so much.

Did they know I was queer? After being asked what year apprentice I was, the next question was, "Are you married?" Prior to 2008, only heterosexuals could marry in California, and I would say, "No." Most read between the lines and moved on. On those rare occasions when someone asked if I was queer, I would reply, "Yes. I'm a dyke." Charlie asked me the first day we met, and word spread on the jobsite.

I was surprised that they did not talk much about their wives or children. They discussed hobbies, cars, the Lakers and the Dodgers, and what they watched on television, which was right up my alley. I knew they had wives who took care of them, just as tía Mincy dedicated her life to taking care of Mando. I rarely asked about their personal lives, mostly because I did not want them asking me about mine and because I was not that interested in getting to know much about them. But I did ask them about where they lived in Los Angeles, where they had been raised, and how they got to be electricians.

Electricians often boasted about how good we were as a team. We would cheer with and for each other when our labor resulted in a floor of lights getting turned on, or when a motor we connected roared for the first time. Safety precautions prevented us from playing music or wearing headphones on jobsites (although I would often try to get away with it), but a few electricians liked to sing. When Charlie could foretell our job was getting close to the end, he started singing Willie Nelson's "On the Road Again." I learned the chorus and sang along.

Slim also seemed to come around. He never spoke to me, but I watched him observe me a couple of times. After I had worked diligently for a few months, he gifted me a new metal file. Each time I cut a metal support, I needed to file the edges, and I had been using the company's file. He approached me and said, "You are doing a good job. Here, I brought you a new file." I took it, and he said, "It's for you. I want you to keep it." He could tell I appreciated the gift, even though I only said, "Thanks." I figured it was the closest thing to an apology I would ever get from Slim, and I ended up treasuring that file. When the Hughes Corporate Headquarters job came to an end, AMELCO laid off Charlie but transferred me to one of their other jobs, constructing Parkview Plaza in Manhattan Beach. Slim needed to have recommended my transfer, but I never saw him again.

Maybe it was the union ethic or the fact that I was the only woman, but during my apprenticeship, most electricians were rather protective of me and invested in ensuring my success. The idea of a brotherhood meant something to them, and some expressed this to me. They advised me not to outwork older electricians or make them look bad, and to always work for the collective good of the union. On construction sites, electricians were paid more than the other tradespeople and were considered the most skilled. I would be harassed for being queer by men in the other trades, like drywallers and laborers, but there was a collegiality among electricians. I cannot point to a time when an electrician refused to work with me or tried to undermine me.

When a structure or building was completed, I moved on, and I appreciated that aspect of the trade. I always met new people (albeit straight men), and each job required me to perform different tasks. I was constantly challenged, learning new skills, or operating new machinery and

FIGURE 3.7 Author at work as an electrician in 1985. Private collection of author.

power tools. I appreciated the men, whose names I cannot remember but who were mostly white, who helped me during my apprenticeship. They took the time to teach me which pliers to use on a specific task, and one went as far as taking my hand and placing each of my fingers on a pair of tongue-and-groove pliers to ensure I held them correctly. Most were willing to share their knowledge of the trade with me so that I would rise to become a peer who, in a few years, would pass on the skills to new apprentices and earn as much money as they did. I never formed friendships with the men I worked with, and outside of the jobsite, our paths never crossed. I was a Brown queer who sought spaces of belonging out in the world, but as an electrician, I found spaces through Local 11 that allowed me to perform the duties and work that I enjoyed and loved.

CHAPTER 4

Sticking Together Like "GLLU"

I n 1983, I made the fateful decision to attend the First National Lesbians of Color Conference. Within hours of my arrival I met three bold Chicanas; they introduced me to a group in L.A. that I had never heard of: Gay and Lesbian Latinos Unidos (GLLU). I ended up joining the group and remained active in it for the next ten years. Until then, I had only met gay Latino men on dancefloors. Those I met in GLLU were warm, openhearted, and around my age. We shared similar cultural upbringings and a political consciousness that prioritized immigrant issues and supporting the United Farm Workers.

David Gonzáles, at only thirty years old, held the distinction of being first GLLU president. He was raised in Los Angeles, and he lived and breathed Dodger Blue. In 1984 he learned that if we bought so many tickets to the Dodgers game, perhaps as many as 30, our group's name would appear on the stadium's diamond-vision screen. David purchased the tickets, which were around $5.00 each, and we reimbursed him. I never asked if he was fully reimbursed—he likely was not.

It was a 1:00 p.m. game, and the sun was so strong that even those with browner skin got sunburns. Fernando Valenzuela was pitching, and Fernandomania was sweeping the nation. As the author and journalist Gustavo Arellano reminds us,

> Mexicans who came of age in the 1980s were part of the first generation that truly felt comfortable on both sides of the Mexican-American hyphen. Valenzuela was just an affirmation of who we were becoming. To see him dominate in the American pastime showed we could win in this country as unapologetic mexicanos too. We didn't need to subscribe to

the victim narratives too long attached to us in the Southland and beyond by outsiders and ourselves alike.[1]

That afternoon, we witnessed the words "Gay and Lesbian Latinos Unidos" appear on the large screen. They hung suspended in the air for less than thirty seconds. For a moment, we remained collectively and silently awestruck. Then we burst out cheering, pointing to the screen, and celebrating in the aisles in contagious joy. Close to 55,000 people, mostly Brown people, were in the stadium that day, and many of them could not help but notice Gay and Lesbian Latinos Unidos on the diamond-vision screen. Those who sat near our group heard the commotion and checked for what they had missed. Some people were puzzled, but many others cheered with us.

Living in a world that refused to accept us, we sought to legitimize ourselves and our right to exist through a variety of acts and organizing efforts. Some may question if projecting "Gay and Lesbian Latinos Unidos" on the screen at Dodger Stadium challenged homophobia, racism, or restrictive immigration policies, but this small act brought us joy and was collectively empowering. It made us stronger and more united. Amid the alienation and isolation Brown queers often experienced, we would often remind ourselves that we were GLLU and "stuck together." We cultivated opportunities and interests that brought us closer together and kept us working as a group. Without the fun, celebration and camaraderie, GLLU would not have endured to ignite a new era of Latine queer organizing in the 1980s.

I did not fully integrate myself into GLLU until 1986, when I completed my electrician apprenticeship program. Before that, I was working a forty-hour week and attending required evening classes. All of my classmates in District 3 were white and male. I was the oldest in my class, the only woman and the only person of color. Tom Gonzales was light skinned and white identified.[2] The young men in my class had attended local schools and married their high-school sweethearts. Typically, their father or a close male family member had been an electrician; in a few cases, they were related to someone who owned an electrical contracting firm. I attended classes with the same guys for four years. We maintained cordial relationships, but I remained in the background. I bonded most with Mike, a handsome, single, super-masculine guy who tended to be loud and extroverted. We sat in the back of the classroom, in the last row of seats. He had no problem carrying on loud conversations with someone across the room. Sitting next to him made me feel less different, and I appreciated that he would always turn his body in my direction and speak softly when he talked to me.

My classmates never asked me if I was queer, and I did not offer the information. During our class breaks, they would huddle around each other outside and talk. I stayed inside, did some stretches, and rested. Most of my classmates socialized after class, but I hurried home.

Mike disappeared in the third year because he was behaving erratically at his job site. We found out he was addicted to cocaine, which explained why he would show up at our apprenticeship classes ready to dive into whatever the topic was, engage with the instructor, and ask endless questions. Like me, most of the others were wiped out. A few times, Local 11 held mandatory classes to warn us about the dangers of cocaine and its highly addictive nature. A police officer once stunningly ended his presentation by saying, "Don't try cocaine. Because if you do, you will like it. No, you will love it." The class roared. I sat next to Mike, who was cheering, not knowing he was probably high.

After Mike went to rehabilitation, the union allowed him to return and complete his last year with the class after ours. I never saw him again, but a few years after I completed the apprentice program, one of my work partners told me about a guy on his last job site who everyone called "The Animal." He said that this electrician pushed metal pipes through walls with unusual force, carried double loads on his shoulders, and worked at an incredible pace. The Animal was also loud. I asked my coworker if he knew his actual name, and found out it was Mike. He had most likely relapsed. In the 1980s, cocaine seemed to be everywhere.

Because I never worked at a particular construction site for more than a few months, I sometimes encountered familiar faces at new job sites. Nicknames like "The Animal" were pretty common in the trade and sometimes followed you to a new job site. I could see how someone who was the spitting image of Hoss from the television series *Bonanza* received his nickname, but I never bothered to figure out where random nicknames like Big D came from.

During my apprenticeship, Tom Gonzales and I were often assigned to the same job site. First year apprentices were often referred to as cubs, which I did not mind, but in later years, when the electricians found out that Tom and I were in the same class, they started calling him Bam-Bam and me Pebbles, after the characters in *The Flintstones*. Tom hated it because it implied we had romantic feelings toward each other. He would protest and shout, "I'm married!" or, "She doesn't even like men!" I did not care about that aspect, but I secretly would have preferred being called Bam-Bam. At some point toward the end of my apprentice, someone started calling me Peppermint Patty, after the androgynous character from the Peanuts gang. As far as nicknames were concerned, Peppermint Patty did not bother me as much when I considered the alternatives.

I started to feel less connected to LOC after I helped organize the group's 1981 Halloween Dance. It was a successful and well-attended fundraiser. At the next LOC meeting, I asked how much money we raised and was scolded for doing so. The lack of transparency regarding financial matters bothered me, and I stopped attending the group's meetings. The next year, they put out professionally designed promotional materials for the First National Lesbians of Color Conference at the Cottontail Ranch in Malibu. It seemed out of character for LOC because the group had never discussed staging a national conference before. I assumed new women and energy had spearheaded the effort and had done most of the planning.

On September 8, 1983, Irene Martínez and I set out for Malibu to attend the conference. Owned by Pepperdine University, the Cottontail Ranch was a 23-acre summer camp and retreat center in the Santa Monica Mountains. It included a number of rustic cabins and could house up to 250 people.[3] Other lesbian groups had held retreats there, because its secluded location offered all-women gatherings an additional layer

FIGURE 4.1 First National LOC Conference program cover, 1983. Private collection of author.

of safety. I brought my camera to take photos. That and everything else I needed for the weekend fit in a backpack.

More than 200 lesbians of color were expected to attend the conference. Irene and I were some of the first ones to arrive. Tables were being set up, some of them definitely political, like the "Free Meryl Woo" table. The University of California at Berkeley had fired Woo, a Marxist feminist and writer, and she retaliated by filing a lawsuit charging the university with discrimination.

Later that afternoon, a new cabinmate, Tommy Escárcega, a bicultural and binational Chicana from El Paso, joined us. She spoke with an authoritative voice and had a sharp political mind. Although we were out in nature, Tommy wore men's formal clothing: an ironed dress shirt and pants. Irene and I were smitten with Tommy. When her friends Geneva Fernández and Laura Esquivel arrived, I became infatuated with them too. All of us instantly connected. They were part of the Gay and Lesbian Latinos Unidos (GLLU) and were intent on recruiting more women to join the group.

I found the idea of joining a group that recognized Tommy, Laura, and Geneva as leaders enticing. The fact that they were all Chicanas made bonding with them easy. It was like we already knew each other—which in Geneva's case was true. We had not seen each other in nearly twenty years, but flickers of recognition kept going off in my mind once we met. Initially, I attributed it to having so much in common. After a few months, I told her that I spent my summers in Boyle Heights as a child and stayed with my aunt on Boulder Street. That is when Geneva and I connected the dots, pointed to each other, and said, "That was you!"

I stayed close to the GLLU women the entire weekend at the conference. I wandered in and out of the main building and sessions, and only attended the large session for Latina lesbians, facilitated by Gloria Anzaldúa. This session was not on the program, and handwritten flyers announced the meeting time and place. Written works by Chicana feminists were in the early stages, and until this point, Gloria Anzaldúa was known for co-editing the pathbreaking anthology, *This Bridge Called My Back: Writings by Radical Women of Color* with Cherríe Moraga in 1981. Her celebrated book, *Borderlands/La Frontera: The New Mestiza* was years away from being released.

Most of the thirty or so Latina lesbians at the session were familiar with Anzaldúa's work. We listened to her share consejos (advice) in devoted attention. Many took notes as she talked about dismantling patriarchy and emphasized how radical Latina lesbian sexual expressions and relationships were to the larger society. A blond-haired blue-eyed Latina brought up that she did not feel accepted as a woman of color at the conference. Gloria listened patiently but did not say much. Others were not so kind, insisting that this was not the time nor the place for the white Latina to try to work out that issue. She started crying, has-

FIGURE 4.2 Latina lesbian hugging circle at the LOC Conference. Gloria Anzaldúa (right) in light colored shorts and white tank top, 1983. Photograph by author.

tening the workshop's end. As a final activity to conclude the session, someone suggested a hugging circle. Gloria praised us and asked us to rejoice. As she and the group started to link hands, I moved away and took photos.

After the large session, perhaps because it ended rather abruptly, Gloria Anzaldúa sat under a tree and held one-on-one sessions with those who wanted to talk to her. Despite a long line, everyone was considerate and it moved quickly. As I awaited my turn, I debated what type of advice to seek. When I sat down across from Gloria, I offered, "I do not know how to feel okay with myself in the world." "You need to write," she said. "This is the most important thing we can do." She must have seen the blank expression come across my face because she queried, "Okay?" "Yes, thank you," I replied, and walked away. At that time, in 1983, writing about my Brown and queer experiences seemed like the last thing I had the time or the energy to do. To my knowledge, despite her countless essays, Gloria Anzaldúa never wrote about the 1983 conference. After the one-on-one sessions, I did not see her again at the conference.

Criticisms of the conference and LOC for not being political enough and for dedicating too much time to discussing "personal identity, spirituality and self-growth" circulated after the conference. One claimed that "it shortchanged those women who came for serious political discussion." The LOC Conference may have disappointed a few people or failed to mount a national plan to "defeat the right wing, capitalism and the patriarchy," but the fact that some who met at the conference moved forward and organized on the local level, as those from GLLU did, should not be dismissed.[4]

Many of the gay Latinos who founded GLLU in 1981 had been active in Movimiento Estudiantil Chicano de Aztlán (M.E.Ch.A) student groups.[5] Influenced by Chicane, women's, and gay movements, the small group of men who founded GLLU sought to liberate themselves from the homophobic, patriarchal, and cultural restraints of the past. They extolled the virtues of being queer and the way they lived their lives. They—as would all the new members like myself—refused to dilute their queerness for other Latines or dilute their brownness for whites. The group formed as Gay Latinos Unidos, but once Geneva became an active member, they decided that a cogender group better fit their political goals and started the Lesbian Task Force to focus their efforts on recruiting more women into the group. Men were active members in that committee.

GLLU's main meeting, or General Assembly, took place on Thursday evenings at 7:00. The president typically chaired the meeting in accordance with Robert's Rules of Order and strictly adhered to the agenda. All committee chairs and cochairs were expected to inform the general membership of their activities. The secretary took minutes. Before the internet and email, those active in GLLU were constantly meeting for breakfast and late dinners to discuss ideas with each other, to ponder different approaches to problems, and of course to gossip. I do not remember cooking many meals during my most active years in GLLU, in the second-half of the 1980s, because it seemed that I often needed to talk over GLLU business with others at the Crest coffee shop in Silver Lake or Barragan's in Echo Park.

Electing officers according to GLLU's bylaws helped keep the group on track. If a member did not like someone's politics and approach, they would not vote for them. The president represented the group. If an outside group or the media needed to contact or interview someone from GLLU, they were directed to speak to the president. This also discouraged others who sought influence from speaking for the organization. Before the group ultimately disbanded in 1994, to my knowledge there were two occasions when the organization faced threats. One was when two former leaders came to a meeting and sought to take over the group, around 1986, and another was when an existing president sought to disband the group. Both times, the members voted against those initiatives.

The bond I formed with the other Chicanas I met at the LOC conference continued to grow, although we lost Tommy when she eventually left Los Angeles. The optimism we felt after the LOC Conference was unbridled. We brainstormed and put together a series of rap groups to attract other Latinas. We did not offer a conference ourselves, but instead launched a series of discussion groups at "the Center"—the Gay and Lesbian Community Services Center at 1213 N. Highland Avenue, north of Santa Monica. I had never been inside the Center before that, but Laura and Geneva worked there. Each week new women trickled into the rap group sessions.

In 1984, the Lesbian Task Force decided to change the committee's name to Lesbianas Unidas (LU). To ensure a collective decision-making space for Latinas separate from the men, we declared that only Latinas could participate in LU. To my knowledge, this move never raised concerns with the gay men. LU's core consisted of Geneva, Laura, Irene, and I. Vicki Delgadillo, whom we met at the conference, had recently moved to the L.A. area and also joined us. A few weeks after LU was established, Sylvia, who was born in Peru, also became active in our group. LU met in the late morning on Saturdays to accommodate my schedule.

We did not try to hide how much joy we brought each other. After our Saturday LU meetings, we ate lunch and spent hours getting to know each other further. We would go home for a few hours before getting together again at a club that night. Our club of choice was the Club Flamingo, at 3626 Sunset Boulevard in Silver Lake. In 1983, it advertised itself as "The Party Bar for the L.A. Woman and her friends."[6] It used to be a nightclub and dated back decades. In 2023, it operates as Bacari Silverlake, a higher-end bar and restaurant.

The vast majority of women at the Flamingo were around our age and Brown. Although it did not have a large dance floor, it had a lusciously green outside patio. We would claim a table outside and take turns dancing with each other inside. At that time, the Flamingo's patio was a rare smoke-free option, because laws banning smoking in clubs and bars did not get passed until 1998.

Although Geneva was a diehard Flamingo patron, we would sometimes go to the Catch or Robbie's in Pomona. We never considered clubs in the white boys' town of West Hollywood, although we met some of the guys at Circus Disco on Las Palmas Avenue and Santa Monica Boulevard a few times. The club's owner, Gene La Pietra, supported GLLU and allowed the group to hold some fundraisers there. Circus was a favorite for Brown gay men, but most of the women at the club were straight and only there to party with their gay friends. I always felt welcome at Circus, but the club was huge, and it was easy to lose the friends you arrived with.

Robbie's was further away, at 390 East Pomona Mall Street, but much bigger and flashier than the Flamingo. The club sometimes featured live performances by celebrities like Bonnie Pointer, who was breaking away from the Pointer Sisters and trying to become a solo act. Most of the LU women carpooled or arrived at Robbie's at the same time. After a while, the drive to Pomona did not seem that far. Almost a decade earlier, in 1975, the club we knew as Robbie's was one of the first to play salsa and feature live salsa bands and recording artists, like Luisito Rivera and Ray Medina.[7] The management at Robbie's became familiar with us and allowed LU to host a few fundraisers at their club.

The disc jockey at Robbie's played Sheila E's "The Glamorous Life" a few times a night. Most of us enjoyed dancing to the song and shouted our revised version of it, substituting "feminist" for "glamorous":

She wants to lead the feminist life.
She don't need a man's touch.

She wants to lead the feminist life.
Without love it ain't much.

Sometimes I overanalyzed the lyrics of songs. After mulling over "In My House" by the Mary Jane Girls—

So when you need some lovin' tenderness
And it's me baby that you miss
Here's the key to unlock the door
To my house (to my house)

—I commented to Geneva, "I can't relate to this song because I don't have a house." Geneva pulled me close to her and whispered in my ear, "Lyd, every woman has a house," and gave me a knowing smile.

Until the Flamingo closed its doors sometime in 1985, you could count on most of the LU women to meet up again on Sunday afternoons like clockwork. To entice patrons, the Flamingo set up a grill and offered free hotdogs and hamburgers. In 1984, the club attempted to stage women's wet t-shirt contests. I found them disturbing; like most of the patrons, I was more interested in the free food. Although there was never a short-age of women willing to judge the contest or throw pails of water at the contestants, there was often a lack of women who wanted to enter the challenge, especially on chilly or windy afternoons. A sprinkling of women enjoyed the contest and acted raucously, but most of us just focused on the conversations going on at our tables. The wet t-shirt contests were short-lived.

My involvement with LU and spending so much time in the company of other women of color forced me to make an important decision regarding my relationship with Shirl. She did not mind me being out, but there were nights I wanted to stay out. Never inclined to go behind her back or lie, I was honest. After we split, Shirl continued to support me, and we remain close friends to this day. When I left Venice in 1984, I felt strong. I had bought a new long-bed pickup, and I was part of a group of Chicanas who were full of energy and spoke their minds. My future felt boundless, and I felt secure that life would be kind to me.

In 1984, I moved into a sprawling suburban house in Encino. I rented the section originally designated as "servants' quarters" when it was built. It had its own entrance and fit a queen-size bed and a love seat that faced a wall of shelving where my television sat. I had a small closet and my own bathroom. A door opened into the kitchen, which led to the rest of the house. The owners were two older lesbians, a Latina and a white woman, and I paid them $350 a month rent. The backyard included a swimming pool surrounded by a high wall that ensured privacy. I also had access to a room with a pool table. With the owners' permission, I sometimes invited friends over and had small parties, and a few women swam and laid out naked.

During my year or so in Encino, I lived less than a mile from Michael Jackson, who was at the peak of his career. Every time I needed to get into or out of my quarters, I had to drive past the Jackson family compound on Hayvenhurst Avenue. Even in the wee hours or when it rained, a crowd of fans huddled outside the estate's large gates. Cars and limousines would occasionally pull slowly into and out of the estate, and I would often slow down to watch fans sifting through and diving into the family's trash cans, looking for souvenirs.

The first official cogender event I attended was the GLLU retreat, on April 27, 1984. I enjoyed meeting my gay brothers, and everyone there seemed in high spirits. At our larger session, "Latinas-Latinos Working Together," we collectively strategized on how to tear down sexual, social, and geopolitical borders. The group dynamics impressed me, and there was a lot of laughter. I remember Roland Palencia halting the discussion and saying, "Lydia, what do you think?" I replied, "I don't really know. I work with all guys but never organized with them." He said, "Well, what do you think?" "I'm really liking it," I said, and I remember the men smiling and looking relieved. Even though I attended all the LU meetings, I did not attend GLLU meetings, because my apprenticeship classes kept me busy on weekday evenings. This caused a few of them to mistake me for a separatist who did not want to be around men.

FIGURE 4.3 LU at GLLU retreat, 1984. Photograph by author.

At this retreat, the women set a time to meet. Thirteen of us sat around a circular firepit sharing how much we valued spaces that fostered deep feelings of belonging. At one point, Laura Esquivel asked, "Why don't we organize retreats like this for Latina lesbians?" I distinctly remember a pause before the joyous clapping as we all recognized our next move. I took a few photographs of that session. I regret that I am not in them, but an empty space marks where I sat before I stepped out to take the pictures.

The next week, LU moved to organize the first Latina Lesbian Retreat. We did not fret about the logistical aspects. We used GLLU's connections and funds to reserve Camp Radford in the San Bernardino Mountains near Big Bear Lake, the same retreat center that housed the cogender retreat, about a hundred miles from Los Angeles. At that point, LU had zero dollars in the coffers, and we knew we needed to fundraise for the retreat. We prepared the registration materials and made sure to highlight that the retreat was a "clean and sober" event. The agreement we signed with the City of Los Angeles, who owned Camp Radford, included an "alcohol free" clause, and this aligned with our preferences for the retreat to be a sober space. We also made a point of discussing sobriety issues at the retreat.

We put flyers all over the city, in queer bookstores and bars that Latinas patronized, and we published a short piece in the GLLU newsletter, *Unidad*. Each week we awaited a response. Our biggest worry was whether others would show up. We crossed our fingers and waited for what seemed like months for someone to return their registration materials. GLLU received its mail at the Center, and when an envelope addressed to LU arrived, Geneva alerted us by phone. When we met on Saturday, Geneva brought the envelope and placed it on the living room table. Someone said, "Maybe it is just a woman wanting more information?" Vicky picked the envelope up and slowly opened it. When she pulled out a check for us to see, we cheered and danced around the room. "It's from someone named Cookie!" she exclaimed. We fell into each other on the couch, and I kicked my legs in the air, laughing while yelling, "Cookie!"

Our first Lesbianas Unidas retreat took place in October 1984. We modeled it after the cogendered GLLU retreat. Each attendee had to sign up for a work shift that included either food preparation, cooking, or clean up. I do not remember any friction emerging from the kitchen, although a few times some women avoided signing up for a shift. For weeks before the retreat, we planned out the meals. Every LU member took responsibility for a meal, bought the food, and hauled it to the retreat.

The first few years, I would stop at the East L.A. Market on Whittier Boulevard across from Ruben Salazar Park to buy patas, panza, nixtamal, and the fixings, so that everyone at the retreat could wake up to menudo on Sunday morning. My tía Mincy considered it the best carnicería. I also bought loads of Mexican bread and pastries from La Mascota on Whittier, because that was her bakery of choice. The butcher at the carnicería always commented on the enormous amount of menudo fixings I purchased on Friday afternoon before heading out to Big Bear. He would say, "You must be planning one big party." Once, instead of simply saying, "I am," I replied, "Yeah, a huge party for a bunch of lesbians." I could see the surprise in eyes, but he gave me a knowing nod.

Each year we had sessions on relationships, organizing, and networking, but LU also made a point of including sessions that dealt with coming out to our families and in general, because those were often sites of trauma for Latina lesbians. The first retreat formed a pivotal support network that LU built upon through the years. In addition to workshops, we held Cultural Night on Saturdays, which included performances and readings, and was followed by a dance. Many women formed longtime friendships, and a few found romance.

LU held an annual retreat until the mid-1990s. Most of the women who attended were from Southern California, but Latina lesbians from other parts of the county also attended. We were strict about two aspects of the annual retreat. First, we made sure only Latinas were allowed to attend the retreats. A few times, Latinas insisted that we allow their white partners to come to the retreat. LU did not. We tried to address the matter by returning registration materials submitted by white women, but we sometimes needed to be more aggressive. In 1984, a West Hollywood dignitary showed up at the LU retreat. She claimed that she was Latina because she was Italian. About five Latinas escorted her to her car and asked her to leave.

We also made a point of ensuring the event was clean and sober. We wanted to have sober heart-to-heart conversations at our retreats with the women we shared so many intersecting identities with. We were Brown and queer and seeking to meet others like us. In subsequent years, LU retreats served as a yearly source of energy and connection. The empowerment I felt when I met others like me, with whom I shared so many similar cultural experiences, was overwhelming. I also felt less alone in the world.

Geneva and I were born days apart, and we held a joint thirtieth birthday party celebration at my place in Encino. We had plenty of food and desserts at this event. Our guests crowded into the pool room because it was February and cold outside. The dancing got started toward the end, and the night turned in a memorable one, although I do not remember much. Most of the guests spent the night, and in the morning, I woke up on some blankets on the big house's living room floor with Patricia González, one of the women I had followed around Peanuts years before, who had returned from her adventure on women's land. We ended up dating for a few months. Sometimes, when we went out dancing, she indulged me and brought out her punk moves.

Living in Encino was becoming more challenging, though. As an apprentice, I could not quit or choose a job; the Local 11 board decided which apprentice to assign to which job site to ensure they learned different skills. Encino was also far from both my worksites and Silver Lake, where most of the GLLU crowd lived and socialized. So when Shirl called one day to tell me her neighbors were renting their house, I was interested. It had a two-car garage, and Shirl came up with the idea that I could live in the house and sublet the garage to Building Women, who needed additional storage for their tools and supplies. The arrangement made the $750 a month rent more affordable, and I was thrilled about moving back to Venice. The two-bedroom house also had a pool, which, like the one in Encino, I did not use much, because I never learned to

FIGURE 4.4 Thirtieth birthday party invitation, 1985. Created by author.

swim and chlorine aggravates my eczema. But pools did provide the settings for exciting parties. Mike Garcia, an artist I met in GLLU, roomed with me for a while, which helped my finances during a rough patch when I was unable to work.

Everyone at GLLU wanted to show their support for the United Farm Workers (UFW), because the movement had inspired all of us. GLLU members had already forged a close relationship with the UFW before I arrived, and Conrado Terrazas and Frank Mendiola brought the UFW and GLLU closer together. Luis Jacinto, a longtime member and GLLU's "official" photographer, grew up in Bakersfield, and he and his family maintained a close relationship with César Chávez and Dolores Huerta. César Chávez wrote a letter of support to GLLU in 1982, and the next year, Dolores Huerta and others marched with GLLU in the Christopher Street or Pride Parade. In GLLU circles, that day stands out as one of the group's highlights, because the UFW took such a deliberate and open stance of solidarity with us.

Of course, marching in Pride Parades involved a lot of planning. Everyone in GLLU recognized that we were representing Latines. GLLU always tried to organize around a theme, and there had to be music.

FIGURE 4.5 UFW marching with GLLU at LA Pride, 1983. Photograph by Louis Jacinto.

It also needed to be loud. We contracted a truck, typically one with a flatbed, to carry the humongous speakers. We marched to a different song each year, including Celia Cruz's "La Vida Es un Carnaval" and, of course, Gloria Estefan's "Conga." One year, around 1987, GLLU marched to "El Gran Varón," written by Omar Alfanno and performed by Willie Colón, which told the story of a person with AIDS and the familial and societal stigma she endured.

Brown people lining the parade route lit up when they saw us and our banner and heard the music. Some would run out to take our photo or hug us. That type of effusive support and open expression of pride energized all of us. When I carried the banner, I felt like a rockstar, because women rushed up to hug me and a few surprised me by trying to kiss me.

Although we took our role in Christopher Street West (CSW) seriously, we never took on a large role in planning or organizing the parade and festival. On the other hand, the multiethnic Sunset Junction Street Fair expected GLLU to be active participants in their two-day event. The junction refers to an area in Silver Lake where Sunset and Santa Monica boulevards venture off into separate directions at Sanborn Avenue. During the street fair, seven blocks were closed along Sunset Boulevard to make room for over 50 community booths, free entertainment, and food vendors. The Sunset Junction Street Fair organizers always assigned GLLU a prominent booth or concession stand that generated funds for our group. Once, we scored the dunking booth. It was hilarious to witness friends unexpectedly fall in the water, but I refused to volunteer, even if it was for GLLU. Soda booths were the most lucrative assignment, and we often got them. Some years, we had two booths.

The Sunset Junction area is notable for its queer history. Queers organized against police harassment at the Black Cat Tavern, on Sunset Boulevard in 1967. These protests are now recognized as predating those that took place at Stonewall in New York City in 1969. In the 1980s, the Black Cat Tavern had become Tabasco's, a bar patronized by mostly gay Latinos. Whether the name referred to a state in Mexico or the owners were playing with the sexual stereotype that associated Latine as "spicy," the bar's name was unquestionably Latine. Back then, we did not know we were partying at a historic site, but we recognized it as an integral part

FIGURE 4.6 José Ramírez at Tabasco's for a Sunset Junction fundraiser, 1982. Photograph by Louis Jacinto.

of Sunset Junction. GLLU also held a few beer bust fundraisers there on Sunday afternoons.

In the 1980s, I considered Sunset Junction a Latine Queer neighborhood. A few blocks east of Tabasco's stood another site that marked the area as ours, Club Flamingo. These two bars were what urban historian Natalia Molina calls urban anchors. They represented more than simply Latine Queers carving out a niche for themselves. Instead, as Molina describes it, we were "cultivating" a site of meaningful community building.[8] In the Sunset Junction area, we openly expressed our Brown queerness, felt secure walking on public sidewalks, and were welcome in coffee shops and bars. In 1989, when GLLU established our first office, we deliberately selected a site in Sunset Junction, because we knew we belonged there.

Every year, GLLU celebrated the anniversary of its founding. It was the organization's largest gathering and primary fundraising event. The anniversary dinners gave us the opportunity to dress up and connect with each other in our finest, just as we had witnessed during weddings and other celebrations in our families. We also gave out awards to people and organizations who supported us and our goals. GLLU had filed the needed paperwork to become a California 501c3 nonprofit organization around the time I joined in June 1983, but we never had major donors. We realized that wealthy Latines were not going to write huge checks to support us, which accounts for why we dedicated so much time to fundraising.

GLLU committed itself to producing a quarterly newsletter called *Unidad*, and the bulk of the group's fundraising efforts were dedicated to covering the printing costs for the bulletin, which we mailed in great numbers to subscribers for $5.00 a year. We also placed stacks of them in bookstores, bars, and social service centers frequented by queer Latines. Louis and David took charge of *Unidad* in the early 1980s. I dropped by their house in Echo Park across the lake a few times to help them work on it. They encouraged me to write a few pieces, and in a few years, I took charge of the newsletter. I also put together the anniversary programs. At that time, we used typewriters, photocopied photos, and cut and pasted items to the pages.

FIGURE 4.7 Jewel Thais-Williams receiving a GLLU Award at an anniversary dinner, 1989. Photograph by Becky Villaseñor.

By 1986, I felt like I had witnessed a critical phase in GLLU's evolution. The LU retreats had reached the limit allowed by the retreat center, and women registered early to ensure they could attend. By then, the three GLLU presidents who had served during its initial and formative years, David Gonzáles, Roland Palencia, and Laura Esquivel, were no longer active in the organization. As they moved on to new ventures, new people joined the ranks of GLLU. Rita Gonzáles, who joined GLLU less than two years prior, served as GLLU president in 1986. She remains active to this day in an organization spawned by GLLU, Bienestar. Valentino Sandoval, Tomás Soto, Laura Duran, Juan Mendez, David Trujillo, Sandy Rubio, Andy López, Michael Cardoza, Pat Martel and many others brought new energy to the group, while stalwart early GLLU members like Louis Jacinto, Geneva Fernández, John Ramírez, Eduardo Archuleta, Irene Martínez, Oscar de la O and myself remained as constant mainstays.

Veronica Flores attended a LU retreat in 1985 and brought new energy to the group. We also formed a bond that lasted decades. She had immigrated to the U.S. from Chile and belonged to a large social network of Latinas in Orange County and Long Beach. LU was rather Chicana-centric when Veronica joined, but she nudged us to be more aware of Latina issues and to include salsa music at events to create an atmosphere more welcoming to Latinas. Veronica brought not only her charisma to LU but also her large circle of Latinas, and participation in LU exploded.

Women active in LU did not need to be active in GLLU. For those women who preferred to organize among themselves, LU provided a space to do so. The majority of women who attended the retreats never attended an LU meeting, but they formed a loyal and enthusiastic base that LU counted on to attend fundraisers and community presentations. Carmen Canto, Linda Rangel, Elena Popp, Patricia Gonzalez, Marcia Gonzáles, Susana Moreno, Grace Rosales, Cathy Grijalva, Carla Barboza, and Aída Pineda joined LU after 1986. Aída drew up a new logo for LU in the late 1980s, and LU formed their own marching contingent, separate from GLLU, at the Long Beach and Christopher Street West Pride marches. They carried their own banner, selected their own music, and even choreographed their own marching routines.

Cultural night at the LU retreats became extravaganzas featuring choreographed routines performed by the California Dancing Raisins—

FIGURE 4.8 LU at Long Beach Pride, around 1988. Courtesy of the Laura Aguilar Trust.

who were popular in television commercials during the late 1980s—drag kings performing Juan Luis Guerra and Juan Gabriel, and a Latina Lesbian Dating Game where the contestants competed for a date. Since its inception, the LU retreat had provided childcare, and in the late 1980s, enough children attended that, under the direction of Susana Brito, they performed skits and read poems to kick off cultural night.

On Sunday nights, the Los Angeles radio station KPFK aired IMRU, a program dedicated to queer programming and political change. In 1986, IMRU sought to diversify their programming and offered GLLU their own radio show. The group jumped at the chance. We used KPFK's studio facilities, and IMRU staff helped us launch our program, titled Radio GLLU. The inaugural program aired on April 27, 1986. Rita González, along with Eduardo Archuleta, took charge of Radio GLLU. They offered news, notices of upcoming events, and interviews with Latine queers with different life experiences. We also integrated live musical performances and poetry in Spanish, in addition to book reviews. My participation in Radio GLLU waivered, but the program continued to air until 1996.

The year also proved monumental for my personal evolution. I completed my apprenticeship program, passed the exam, and became an Inside Wireman. I could be more selective about the jobs I took on, and I

FIGURE 4.9 First day of taping Radio GLLU. Louis Jacinto and author, 1986. Courtesy of Louis Jacinto.

made a conscious decision to refuse to work as part of a crew that built mundane office buildings or hotels. I wanted to be a part of a team that built projects and buildings that I read about in the newspaper, that were influencing Los Angeles's future or making it a better city to live in.

I met artist photographer Laura Aguilar in late 1985, when I lived in Venice. She loved social events, where she keenly observed individual and group dynamics. Laura had not met out, self-assured Brown queers before, and it informed her own coming-out process. The Latina lesbians she met in the mid-1980s influenced her and helped her conceptualize a new project that would present images of strong, self-assured, out Latinas—a type of image the world had yet to see.

Laura included me in the Latina Lesbian Series. Mine was one of the first portraits she took. Two photographs of me made it into the series, "Lydia 1" and "Lydia 2." Lydia 1 was taken late in 1985, in my kitchen in Venice.[9] After taking a few shots, Laura suggested I hold an acoustic guitar I had bought in high school and kept in the living room. Although

I was extremely nearsighted, Laura suggested that I take off my glasses. She captured me surrendering my need to see and simply looking in her direction. She returned the next week with contact sheets and larger prints of her top picks. Laura wanted to include me in the creative process, and she asked my opinion about which shot to include in the series. I told her I liked one in which I am wearing glasses and have my feet up on the counter. She pointed toward the photo of me holding the guitar. "You look sexy in this one," she said, and we laughed. I recognized Laura's gift—it was her project and her call.[10]

Laura asked those she selected for the series to offer some handwritten thoughts about ourselves to complement and add depth to the portraits. I had difficulty writing the few words to accompany my photographs, and I went through a few sheets of the special paper she brought over. At 31, my fascination with transformation comes across clearly. I think my words also indicate an effort to escape categorizations and my propensity to embrace change. Each of the photographs in the Latina Lesbian Series is named after the person featured. Granted, only my first name was used, but in 1986, offering our images and words and signing our names constituted a strong statement about being out and the limited representations of that time.

Laura negotiated with a few bookstores to sell Latina Lesbian Series cards and postcards. It was arresting to see my face on postcards for sale at my favorite bookstore, Different Light in Silver Lake, on those older spinning card racks. One day in late 1986, Laura mailed me a postcard. She felt accomplished to have put the series out there for the world to see, but neither she nor I could have predicted how renowned she would become. The media and cultural studies scholar Richard T. Rodríguez asserts that Laura Aguilar's body of work

> will continue to provide invigorating alternatives to the accepted understanding of the body and its placement at the crossroads of class, ability, sexuality, race, and gender. . . . Her influential photography and videos aim to represent a range of experiences and identities that are continually under the threat of erasure or marginalization. . . . [Her art] promises to endure.[11]

I have a long way to go to be who
I would like to be.
Lessons to learn, things to experience.
I hope I will always change things
that feel wrong, in the world,
and in myself.
Lydia

FIGURE 4.10 "Lydia" Latina Lesbian Series. Photograph by
Laura Aguilar. Courtesy of the Laura Aguilar Trust.

If anyone knew how to throw great parties, it was Geneva. They were
legendary. Cindy, another woman in the Latina Lesbian Series who lived
outside Los Angeles, once happened to show up at one of Geneva's parties.
I found Laura's photo of Cindy wearing a zoot suit quite sexy. Laura did
too. That night, I was intent on making a move. As I sat near the edge of
the couch watching Cindy dance, Rita Gonzáles laughingly leaned into me
and managed to push me off the couch. I reached out with my left hand to

block my fall and felt a sharp pain in the middle of my hand. Despite the incident, I found time to chat to Cindy. I mentioned that I had a house in Venice and that she should allow me to give her a tour of the boardwalk. She agreed, and I hoped for good times ahead, despite the throbbing in my hand. I took a couple of aspirin before bed that night. In the morning, my hand was a bit swollen, but I was intent on spending time with Cindy. I considered it my only chance, which turned out to be true.

We shared a few intimate moments during our outing, but my hand was starting to turn a purplish color the more we walked. When we returned to my house, we sat on the couch and as things became more heated between us, so did the pain in my hand. I finally blurted out, "I think I need to go to the ER." At that moment, she seemed to understand, but apparently, she did not. She never expressed an interest in me again, and my fantasy coupling of Lydia and Cindy from the Latina Lesbian Series never happened.

A friend took me to the ER that Sunday evening. I had broken the hamate bone at the base of my left hand, and I had to wear a plaster cast up to my elbow. A part of me felt relieved to have some time off work, and I qualified for state disability payments. My truck had a stick shift, and I could not hold the steering wheel with my injured hand and shift at the same time, which meant I had to rely on friends to do the shopping and take me to gatherings.

Around that time, I met Raquel Molina at a party. She was tall, with shoulder-length peppered gray hair. She loved to dance, and she did so very well. She worked at UPS delivering packages, and I was impressed by the brown outfit she wore to work. No matter the weather, she never wore the pants—only the brown shorts that showed her long, brown, muscular legs. Raquel was more masculine than the women I typically dated, and I appreciated how she lavished attention on me. I had already injured my left hand when we started dating, and she opened doors for me, insisted on driving, and always asked me where I wanted to go to eat. I remember thinking, "Are these the perks of being a femme?" Once Laura Aguilar met Raquel, she included her in the Latina Lesbian Series too.

Raquel was born and raised in Los Angeles, and although she was nine years my senior, we had more in common than I had imagined. She con-

FIGURE 4.11 "Cindy" (left) and "Raquel"(right) from the Latina Lesbian Series, around 1986. Photographs by Laura Aguilar. Courtesy of the Laura Aguilar Trust.

nected deeply with music, had an astonishing sense of rhythm, and often played congas at parties. I attributed these talents to being closely related to the renowned Chicano singer and songwriter Lalo Guerrero, who was born and raised in Tucson. Before Linda Ronstadt, he was the most famous singer to hail from my hometown. As journalist Karen Peterson writes,

> Guerrero inspired and gave rhythm to generations of Mexican Americans, recording an estimated 700 songs. . . . "Canción Mexicana" is still considered the unofficial anthem of Mexico. . . . His work spanned the decades, from the zoot-suited *pachuco* era of the 1940s to Chicano activism in the 1960s (at one time, his booking agent was famed union leader Cesar Chavez), and everything in-between and beyond.[12]

My mother had shared with me that she and Lalo knew each other as children in the old barrio in Tucson. When Raquel introduced me, I asked if he remembered my mother. He thought about it and asked me, "Did your mother have a lot of sisters?" "Yes," I said. "People from the barrio often referred to them as the 'Robles Girls.' Her name was Chita." "You mother was the oldest?" I said yes, and he replied rather animatedly, "Yeah, I remember her. Tell her I say hello," and smiled. My mother was elated when I called to tell her that I had met Lalo and he remembered her.

Raquel went out on a limb and asked Lalo Guerrero to perform at a GLLU fundraiser. I doubted that he would agree to headline a queer event. Raquel was beaming when she reported, "He said 'okay.' He is doing it!" I was flabbergasted. The famoso Lalo Guerrero was going to headline a GLLU event. "For free?" I asked. "Yes!" she replied jubilantly.

As planned, on November 14, 1987, Lalo Guerrero appeared at our event at the ONE Institute. Raquel was on top of the world. She was the toast of the evening, second only to Lalo, because she had made it all happen. As he began his performance and sang many of his classics, he mentioned Raquel as someone dear to him.

I wore that cast on my left hand for six months. My doctor had no explanation other than, "It sometimes happens." He recommended surgery to fuse the bone together, and I spent the month in Tucson with my mother, who still lived in my childhood home, while I waited for the

*G*ay and *L*esbian *L*atinos *U*nidos

requests the honor of your presence at its

SIXTH ANNIVERSARY
DINNER and AWARDS CEREMONY

Saturday, November 14, 1987

The One Institute

1130 Arlington

Los Angeles, California

———— *SPECIAL GUEST ENTERTAINER* ————
LALO GUERRERO

• $20.00 Donation	• 6:00 Cocktails
• Limited Seating	• 7:00 Dinner
• R.S.V.P. by Nov. 11, 1987	• 8:00 Program
• (213) 665-8852 Louis Jacinto	• 9:00 Entertainment & Dancing

FIGURE 4.12 GLLU fundraiser, 1987. Private collection of author.

insurance company to approve the surgery. Maybe it was being home, Chita's cooking, or the fact that I really rested my hand, but it started to feel better. I knew going back to being an electrician was impossible at the time, because I still could not manipulate pliers and hand tools. I needed something else to do for a living, so I worked as a building inspector for the City of Santa Monica for a short stint. In less than five months, I returned to being an electrician.

The mid-1980s, for me and other Brown queer activists in Los Angeles, was a time of great growth. In GLLU and LU, I found camaraderie and joy, and we found multiple ways to lay claim to our space in the world. Our work brought us to ball games, dances, retreats, parades, concerts, and anniversary dinners. We made ourselves known over a diamond-vision screen, in newsletters, on the radio, and in photographs. And we found joy in celebrating ourselves and each other.

I began this chapter by highlighting a small act that challenged homophobia, and I will end with another example: when GLLU prioritized queering the national mainstream cause "Hands Across America." It took place on Sunday, May 25, 1986. If the goal was to form a continuous human chain across the country, we reasoned that it had to include Brown queers. Through Louis Jacinto and David Trujillo's connections with El Centro del Pueblo, a nonprofit community service agency in Echo Park that paid the registration fees, we staked out a block on Whittier Boulevard in East Los Angeles. Along with national and local elected officials and celebrities such as Yoko Ono and Liza Minnelli, we linked hands and swayed to the theme song while yelling, "We're here and queer!"

FIGURE 4.13 Hands Across America, 1986. Private collection of author.

CHAPTER 5

Aiming for the Sky and Feeling the Lows

During my electrician apprenticeship, I had been assigned companies and jobs. As a journeyperson, I choose which construction projects merited an investment of my labor. I managed to take weeks and sometimes months off from work. Working in what was then labeled a man's job and being a "brother" in a labor union came with not only a hefty hourly wage but also benefits, protections and options. I made around $25.00 an hour in 1986. Never motivated by money, I squirreled away my wages so that I could take off from paid employment to pursue my activist endeavors. When I had arrived in Los Angeles in 1978, I expected unknown challenges and gifts. I did not know how those experiences would take shape, but I always felt the need to stand alongside likeminded Brown and queer activists.

After I became a journeyperson, I sought to reward myself with something special. Growing up in Tucson, I had traveled to Nogales on the other side of the U.S.–Mexico border in the Mexican state of Sonora, but never anywhere else in the country. Going to Mexico City had always been a dream of mine. I wanted to experience the Mexican or Aztec pyramids and temples, but I also did not want to feel like a tourist or an outsider in the country that defined so much of my identity and culture. I saw an article in a lesbian newspaper, *off our backs*, about a transnational exchange program in Mexico for U.S. activists, Mujer a Mujer (Woman to Woman).[1] I applied and received an acceptance letter in the mail a few weeks later. I paid for my transportation and around $300.00 for the ten-day program designed to introduce us to feminists organizing and forming cooperatives in Mexico City.

When I arrived, the entire city was still recovering from the deadly Mexico City earthquake that happened a year earlier. Of course, women were at the forefront of fighting for basic human services and housing. The most affecting sites we visited as part of the Mujer a Mujer exchange program were piles of rubble where women shared stories about the demolished buildings that had been either their former workplaces or their former homes. In some cases, they shared that their bosses sought to salvage pieces of machinery and supplies over helping people that needed medical attention.[2]

The few Mujer a Mujer organizers I met were all white women from the U.S. I became close friends with Elaine Burns, who seemed to lead the program. The organizers knew from my application that I was active in Lesbianas Unidas (LU), and they planned events that allowed me to meet lesbians in Mexico City. Everyone in the exchange program, along with a number of local lesbians, visited a women's coffee house and feminist center called Cuarto Creciente. I knew ordinary Spanish, but these women were talking about Karl Marx, Simone de Beauvoir, and their heroes like Joan of Arc. The stress of not being able to keep up with their Spanish caused severe cramping in my stomach. At that event, I was invited to a lesbian party the next weekend and tried to bow out by saying that I was probably busy, but Elaine promised them that she would take me there.

The night of the party, about four women pulled me into an organizing huddle. They wanted LU to be an integral part of an encuentro (gathering) of lesbians they were planning the next year. I expressed interest on LU's behalf, and Lourdes and Alida, two of the leaders who were also in a relationship, insisted that I have lunch with them the next day so they could share more. They were active in "Latina Americana Lesbiana" or LAL, the collective organizing the Encuentro.[3]

When the cab dropped me off for lunch, a servant, who had the same skin color as mine, opened the door and later served us our meal. I was shocked that Lourdes and Alida had a servant. After our meal, they shared some materials that they wanted me to present to LU, because they needed a U.S. contact for the Encuentro. I immediately volunteered to be the contact and dismissed the class differences I had just witnessed by saying to myself, "Not everyone in LAL has servants." By then, I had served as LU cochair since it started, and I felt like the group was more than ready to take on this type of international or hemispheric collaboration.

When I returned to Los Angeles, I called a special LU meeting to discuss the proposal. The group was receptive and excited about being part of a transnational coalition with their Mexicana, Caribbean, and Latin American sisters. LU requested more information, and within weeks, the organizing committee in Mexico City sent a representative, Bárbara, to provide more details. LU formally committed to the project and promised to fundraise to ensure its success. Bárbara also left the banking information we would need to deposit funds directly into the LAL account. In the meantime, the money LU raised was held in the Gay and Lesbian Latinos Unidos (GLLU) general account.

LU went into overdrive planning for the Encuentro and felt honored to collaborate with LAL. We contacted Estilita Grimaldo, who owned and managed Womantours Travel Agency, and she agreed to be LU's official travel agent for the Encuentro.[4] She was able to purchase tickets to Mexico City at a group rate that lowered our fares. We also encouraged other Latina lesbians attending the Encuentro to book their travel though Womantours, and Estilita promised to donate at least fifty percent of her profits towards supporting the Encuentro.

Around this time, on November 22 and 23, 1986, GLLU sponsored the International Lesbian and Gay People of Color Conference, which attracted approximately 300 attendees. LU took advantage of the large gathering. I, along with others, offered a workshop called "The Lesbian Feminist Experience in Mexico" to generate excitement and inform Latina lesbians from other parts of the country about the Encuentro. This is where I first met writer Marianna Romo Carmona, who was in the midst of forming the Latina Lesbian group Las Buenas Amigas in New York City. I also met Gracelia Sánchez and Gloria Ramírez, who went on to establish the Esperanza Peace and Justice Center in San Antonio. All of them attended the Encuentro in Mexico City. It also should be noted that we used GLLU's media resources, such as the newsletter *Unidad* and Radio GLLU, to promote the Encuentro and its related fundraisers.

There were many LU fundraisers for the Primer Encuentro de Lesbianas Feministas de Latinoamérica y el Caribe Conference, which required hours of volunteer labor and ingenuity, but three events were particularly successful. Veronica Flores, a former hair stylist, organized the first. She called every hairdresser she knew and organized a Cut-a-Thon at Sunset Junction. GLLU members and supporters showed up to support the effort, and so did many who attended the Sunset Junction Street Fair. The booth was busy around the clock, and all the hairstylists volunteered their time. I never expected it to be such a success. LU raised over a thousand dollars.

LU members Raquel Molina and Carla Barboza coordinated the second fundraiser for the Encuentro: they brought Sinigual, an all-woman salsa band, to Los Angeles. Their performance was a first, because a live all-women salsa band had *never* before performed in the Los Angeles

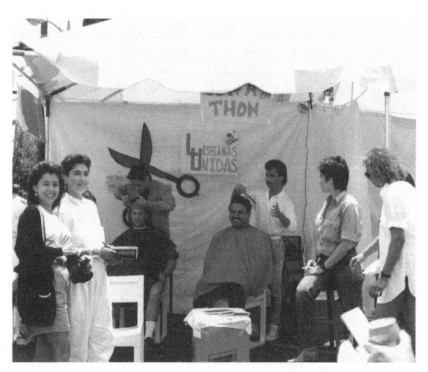

FIGURE 5.1 LU Cut-a-Thon at Sunset Junction, 1987. Left to right: Susana, Marcia, Carla and Raquel. Photograph by author.

FIGURE 5.2 Sinigual fundraising flyer, 1987. Private collection of author.

area. Sinigual requested that LU subsidize their transportation costs but waived their performance fees. We ended up chartering a bus because they needed room for their instruments. To pique interest, weeks ahead of the event, some LU women started distributing flyers to women exiting lesbian clubs. The flyers simply stated, "Sinigual is coming!" They did this randomly at different venues and would not respond when asked "Who is Sinigual?" Tickets to the event were made available to purchase through local bookstores. When information was released about the all-woman salsa ensemble, there was a rush for Sinigual tickets.

Lastly, LU organized a raffle for a Hawaiian vacation. The winner would be announced at the Sinigual fundraiser. Estilita Grimaldo, who donated more money than she earned as LU's official travel agent, donated the roundtrip airfare and lodging for one week. At the same time, they were planning the Sinigual performance, LU members were also going to clubs and gatherings to sell $5.00 tickets to the raffle.

On October 13, 1987, I crowded into a bus taking us to the Primer Encuentro de Lesbianas Feministas de Latinoamérica y el Caribe. It was held in a "secret" large retreat center in Cuernavaca, a little more than fifty miles south of Mexico City. It seemed like a dream come true. Just as I had imagined, the bus was packed with lesbians from the Dominican Republic, Chile, Argentina, Peru, and even Cuba and Nicaragua.

LU had raised around $9,000 for the Encuentro. In 2023 dollars, that would be a little more than $24,000. We wired the funds we raised directly to the LAL organizers. Some of the women who directed the fundraising efforts did not attend because of work conflicts. Estilita Grimaldo of Womantours Travel Agency offered LU one free roundtrip flight to Mexico City. The group unanimously voted to offer it to Laura Aguilar, who was an active LU member at the time, because we wanted her to participate in this historic gathering and display her photographs from the Latina Lesbian Series. Eight active LU members attended the Encuentro, and except for the $86 we each received from a special LU fundraiser designed for our travel expenses, each of us paid for our transportation costs and expenses.[5]

A few of us, including Laura, arrived at the retreat compound during the evening. We were led to a large kitchen and told that we would be sleeping on the floor. Women kept arriving throughout the night, we did not have enough blankets—I do not remember being advised to bring a sleeping bag, so I did not—and the floor was cold. LAL often communicated that it needed more money, and as I lay on the floor, I thought these were the best accommodations they could secure, and that everyone who attended the Encuentro would be sleeping on the floor.

In the morning, the first official day of the historic gathering, I scoped out the retreat center's layout in the daylight. A five-foot wall surrounded the complex, ensuring privacy, and a number of small studio units lined the side. I noticed a blond woman outside drying her hair with a towel and recognized Elaine Burns, the Mujer a Mujer organizer. This made me suspect that the LAL organizers had assigned her a small room. I investigated and confirmed that Elaine and women from Europe who belonged to the Dutch-based International Lesbian Information Service (ILIS) were staying in the small units.

I was livid! Some of the attendance estimates that LAL had previously sent LU mentioned non-Latinas would be attending the Encuentro, but I expected their participation would be minimal and that they would not be so visible. I searched for Lourdes and Alida, because I felt betrayed by my Mexicana sisters. When I found them, I did not say hello but instead yelled, "¡Nos hiciste dormir en el suelo y les diste camas a las güeras!" (You made us sleep on the floor and gave the white women beds!) They seemed shocked and fearful of me. The combination of sleep deprivation and anger led me to issue an ultimatum in Spanish, "I do not care what you do or how you need to do it, but every woman from the U.S. who spent the last six months of their lives fundraising and saving to be at this encuentro is sleeping in a bed tonight." Then I walked away.

At that moment, I did not understand the depth of the Mexicana's connection to their European and white women allies. They had been working with international coalitions who had been funding trips for them to attend conferences in Europe long before they contacted LU. In addition to giving them better accommodations, on the first day, the LAL organizers allowed the European women to lead one of the early sessions.

Some of the other U.S. Latinas were also incensed, and we organized a session for U.S. Latinas. The LAL organizers were surprised when I told them we were meeting separately to discuss the presence of the European and white women at the Encuentro. A Mexicana from LAL offered to attend the session to explain why the European and white women needed to be included, inferring that there was something I did not understand. I replied, "No. The U.S. Latinas will meet on their own."

I facilitated the gathering for the U.S. Latinas. We met outside to ensure we were not disrupting any of the scheduled sessions. Most in the circle spoke English. We tried to process through our anger and frustrations, because everyone in that circle, including myself, wanted the Encuentro to succeed. We strategized on how to connect with the Caribbean and Latin American women we were meeting with and how to move forward and build the lesbian transnational coalition we dreamed of. Since the LAL organizers had invited the European and white women, the U.S. Latinas did not request that they be expelled—but we did demand that the European or white women not be allowed to lead any sessions or discussions. We also did not want them to serve as translators for the U.S. women who did not speak Spanish.

The U.S. Latinas met for around two hours. I asked that others talk to the LAL organizers regarding the presence of the European and white women, so they would know that these sentiments and requests came from the group. Whether the LAL organizers ever discussed the U.S. Latinas' requests with the European and white women is doubtful. They continued to slip in and observe the discussions, enjoyed access to the grounds and cultural performances, and shared their meals with the larger group.

As the day progressed, I noted that more Caribbean and Latin American women were being assigned the small studios. A false sense of loyalty still led me to believe that the LAL organizers would apologize and inform me that they had instructed the white women to exchange places with us because they did not want their Chicana sisters sleeping on the floor. But they were unable to do that. LAL organizers instead booked a block of rooms at a hotel, away from the retreat center, for LU and for some of the other U.S. Latinas to stay at during the conference.

At some point, a few LAL organizers proposed excluding Chicanas and U.S. Latinas from expressing ourselves and voting in a new Caribbean and Latin American collective we were in the midst of forming. I have deep admiration for women like Elena Popp, Mariana Romo-Carmona, Veronica Flores, Gracelia Sánchez, and others, who were much more fluent in Spanish than me and who persevered and persistently showed up to challenge assumptions about U.S. Latinas having "first-world" en-

FIGURE 5.3   Author (back row, left) with some of the U.S. Latinas at the Encuentro, 1987. Courtesy of the Laura Aguilar Trust.

titlements and privilege. Chicana scholar Yvonne Yarbro-Bejarano, who attended the Encuentro, deduced that the "experience [of attending the Encuentro] did remind us that many Latin American women do not have a full understanding of the racism and classism, the social, linguistic and cultural discrimination that define the reality of Latinas and Chicanas living in the U.S."[6]

Many parallel agendas were taking place at the Encuentro. As organizational issues were being hammered out, others attended the scheduled sessions on identity, monogamy, mothering, and relationships. I could tell those sessions generated much interest and enthusiasm, because I often heard laughter coming from those sessions. Others frolicked in the pool, and a few actively engaged in seducing one another.

Past organizing history and divisions between the Mexico City lesbians also detonated at the Encuentro. A Marxist feminist claimed that the LAL had expelled her and insisted on airing her grievances. By this time, I had stopped attending the organizational meetings and had joined the regular sessions. Since she considered me a source of funding for the gathering, the aggrieved woman often sought me out to make sure I un-

FIGURE 5.4 Author (center) with U.S. Latinas at hotel in Cuernavaca, 1987. Private collection of author.

derstood her version of the story. I responded by staying away. I started eating my meals at the hotel's outside patio while drinking fifteen-cent beers and engaging in conversations regarding the differences between racism, class, and imperialism with some of the other U.S. Latinas.

A friend from San Francisco had invited some friends, including a Korean American woman named Linda, to come to Mexico with her while she attended the Encuentro. They all ended up staying at the hotel. I had met Linda in Los Angeles once, but she had been in a relationship. I kept running into her at the hotel, and as I purposely distanced myself from the Encuentro, I grew more interested in her. Linda lived in Berkeley, and by the time we returned to the United States, we were officially in a long-distance relationship. When I returned to Los Angeles, a friend remarked, "You went to Mexico and came home with someone who is Korean? How does that happen?"

I returned to the retreat center the day after the Encuentro ended. I wanted to work things out in my head, and perhaps I sought solace. I had gone missing for less than two days, but it felt like much, much longer. The retreat center was empty, but the LAL organizers, including Lourdes and Alida, were still there. They sat at a table surrounded by boxes, sorting piles of papers. I was surprised that they were happy to see me. They expressed relief that they had pulled it off and that there were no major catastrophes. I swallowed my words. None of us had the energy or desire to revisit bad feelings and conflicts. They made me promise that I would stay in touch and that I would return and visit them in Mexico. I promised I would, and thanked them for all the work they put into the Encuentro. We hugged and I never connected with them again.

That LU organized its fundraising efforts leading up to the Encuentro so efficiently and successfully served to heighten my expectations of the event. When I think over what happened, I recognize that those in LAL who organized the Encuentro were taking tremendous personal risks. The harassment directed at them from the state for publicly asserting their lesbianism was more severe than what we generally experienced in the U.S. Also, the women who tried to prevent the U.S. Latinas from fully participating were only a small sector of the organizing committee. In addition, I could not appreciate the Mexicanas' goal and investment in global feminist organizing and networking. That close to two hundred fifty lesbians gathered October 14–17 in 1987 for the historic Encuentro was in itself a tremendous feat.

In general, LU took great pride in the role they played in making the Encuentro a reality.[7] We had started organizing the First National Latina Lesbian Conference before the Encuentro, because we wanted Latinas who had scheduling conflicts or could not afford the expenses involved with traveling to Mexico to attend this alternative gathering. We also assumed there would be momentum to keep going after the Encuentro. LU had distributed early promotional materials and even set a date for the conference. After witnessing some of the organizational misfires at the Encuentro, some of us in LU felt less enthusiastic about moving forward with a national Latina Lesbian Conference. Although we received a $1,500 grant from the Open Meadows Institute, we returned the money, because LU could no longer commit to this type of endeavor. Instead, LU refocused its agenda on local community building. LU also continued to hold its annual retreats, entered into a number of community collaborations, and in 1990 took over the Latina Lesbian Support Group that held weekly peer discussions—one in Spanish and another in English—in East Los Angeles.[8]

After the Encuentro, the owners of the 1926 two-bedroom, two-bathroom home I was renting in Venice decided to sell it. It went for $210,000. I thought the price was outrageous, but, as an indication of skyrocketing home prices, it is now valued at over 1.5 million dollars.

Veronica Flores and I entered a cost-saving agreement and moved into a one-bedroom apartment in Silver Lake, near North Hoover Street and Santa Monica Boulevard. We split the $560 a month rent (which included water) in a newly constructed apartment building on Del Mar Avenue. About six months later, we moved into a rather spacious two-bedroom in the same building. The apartment had a patio, and we each had our own bedroom and private bathroom on opposite ends of the apartment. We paid $720.00 a month for the larger apartment, located in what seemed like the center of Los Angeles, and I started taking on more jobs in the downtown area and in the Hollywood movie studios.

Because I moved from jobsite to jobsite, I got to know Los Angeles pretty well. I was always on the search for shortcuts to avoid sitting on the freeway. In retrospect, moving from one construction project to another also reflected the other parts of my life. The last thing I longed for was a long-term relationship. That entailed time I did not have to spare, because I was always on the move, either organizing the next meeting or on my way to one. My relationship with Linda, who I met at the Encuentro, was short-lived. It was fun at first, but I could not keep up with my expanding travel budget, which included a visit to Tucson at least every two months. Plus, I was too involved in GLLU, and too much was happening in Los Angeles.

In 1988, some of the GLLU guys bought a group of tickets to Linda Ronstadt's performance at the Universal Amphitheatre on February 17 for the first "Canciones de Mi Padre" tour performance in Los Angeles. I had been playing the album around the clock at home. When I arrived at the venue, there was a woman I had never met before with the group.

Before I entered the row, the entire GLLU crowd scooted over and left the seat next to her empty. I introduced myself, and she said her name was Monica. When I asked what she did, she said, "I am a comedian." Just her saying that made me laugh, because this was the first time learning that Chicana lesbian comedians existed. She had been part of a comedy duo in the Bay Area and had recently moved to L.A. to go solo. When Monica Palacios said she loved Linda Ronstadt, I knew that we had, at least in my book, a lot in common.

About a year before I moved to Silver Lake, in 1986, two fires struck the L.A. Central Library downtown. City and corporate leaders moved to put together funding to rehabilitate, restore, and renovate the cherished library.[9] I had gone there as a child with my mother during my summer visits, and it seemed like a magical palace to me. I moved quickly at the chance to be part of the construction crew that would bring the library back to its former glory and beyond. On my first day of work, I witnessed books being packed into boxes and loaded onto trucks at the loading dock. The library staff had been moved to another site. I was lucky not to get assigned to the crew working on the library expansion; instead, I was assigned to work in the most historic and grand sections of the library. I loved arriving at work each day, although my tenure there lasted only about two months. Space-saving shelving systems had already been installed by the manufacturer before my arrival. I added the electrical wiring that powered the shelves to move. I was also the electrician assigned to add the wiring needed for the new children's puppet theater that was added as part of the renovation.

April 18, 1989 marks my first day of work at the Library Towers, located across the street from the Central Library. At that time, it was then the tallest building in Los Angeles and the tallest building west of the Mississippi River. The topping-off party was taking place the morning I arrived. This is when the last steel beam is hoisted up by a crane and set in its place. The media was out in force, and I saw City Councilperson Gloria Molina. The politicians, engineers, and bankers all signed the large beam, but all the workers got to add their names too. I had just gotten there when my Chicano foreman said, "Come on let's go, it's the topping off party." I followed him and stood in line to add my name. Some workers wrote

FIGURE 5.5 U.S. Bank Tower, also known as Library Tower. Photograph by Louis Jacinto.

more than their names, but I simply wrote. "LOTERO" in capital letters. Everyone cheered when the final beam was hoisted into the air and set in place.

At first, I loved working there. I was assigned Ram, an older mellow Chicano who had been raised in East Los Angeles, as my work partner. We were responsible for installing all the electrical lines in the machine rooms on each floor of the Library Towers building. Large heating and cooling units took up most of the space, and because I was younger and more agile, I agreed to climb on top of the units.

Ram would bend and cut the pipe on the ground, then hand me the finished pieces so I could drill the supports and install the conduits up high. While he did that, I lay down and waited. It seemed cool at first, because I wore my headphones and listened to Madonna's "Like a Prayer" over and over. Someone on the jobsite read an article in the *L.A. Times* that reported I headed GLLU. The person who operated the lift—a crude form of an elevator, which I used often at the 73-story building—started referring to me as "Mr. President," which I considered better than my previous nicknames.[10]

About once a month, Ram and I were given the opportunity to work on Saturday, which meant overtime wages. Because we were one of a few workers, we were able to take the lift to the top, where the helicopter pad would eventually be built, to have our lunch. The view of Los Angeles was incredible, and some days we could see the ocean. Ram did not talk much, but we smiled a lot at each other when we were up there. I always felt safe with him. After we ate our lunch, we would lie down, with our bodies pointing opposite directions, and look at the sky in silence. I am sure he was thinking what I was: that we were the luckiest people in Los Angeles. And, in this moment, we were literally on top of the world. Unfortunately, every floor had a machine room, and they were pretty much identical. It took us about a week to complete one. By the time I reached the 25th floor, I hated going to work. Ram said he liked the repetition, but I could not take it, and I quit.

Raised a Catholic, I never considered religion a source of comfort or answers while I was growing up. During a catechism class as a child, since they required I memorize the Apostles' Creed, I asked one of the nuns, "If God has no beginning or end, where did we come from?" (God was always a "he" in the 1960s.) She replied calmly but sternly, "If you believed you would know and would not ask this question." I recognized then that the answer to this origin mystery lay beyond me. I added it to my "unsolvable" list and moved forward. I also placed the question, "Why am I queer?" on that unanswerable list. I knew that trying to answer these two questions would be fruitless, and I empowered myself by moving through the world as a nonbeliever and a queer. However, expressing my sexuality did not place me at an increased risk of acquiring the HIV virus as it did the sexually active gay men of my generation, and I did not need to grapple with my mortality.

Before 1984, even though HIV/AIDS had been around for years, there was a widespread misconception that AIDS was a "white" disease. This fallacy even circulated in the circles I traveled in. In February 1984, GLLU's newsletter *Unidad* reported that in L.A. County, 315 people had died of AIDS. Of these, 30, or a little over 10 percent, were Latino.

I did not realize the gravity of HIV/AIDS until the latter part of 1985, when I met Reverend Carl Bean. He attended a GLLU meeting to share that he had started the Minority AIDS Project (MAP). After the meeting, I introduced myself to the gay African American man of the cloth. He smiled and said, "Call me Rev." He had taken the bus to the meeting, so I gave him a ride home, and we ended up grabbing something to eat. Over dinner, he told me about the many sick gay Latinos at the L.A./ USC County Hospital. "Your group, GLLU has got to wake up," he said. He told me he took the bus to the county hospital every Friday. He also shared that he was trying to learn Spanish, and that it would help him to have someone like me go with him to help translate. I warned him that my Spanish speaking skills were pretty marginal, and he responded,

"Well, they are better than mine!" For the next few months, I picked up the Rev on Friday nights around 6:30, and we spent around two hours at the L.A./USC County Hospital. Until then, I had read about HIV/AIDS, but I did not know anyone who had died from it. I knew that one of the GLLU founders, José Ramírez, was sick with HIV/AIDS and had left Los Angeles to be with his family, but that was the extent of my personal connection with the disease.

I brought flowers the first time I picked up the Rev. It warmed his heart, but I never did it again. When we arrived at the hospital, I sensed desperation even before we walked inside the imposing but aging structure. In the waiting room, most sat or slumped on the floor. I slowly followed behind the Rev as we moved through the hallways. The flowers in my hand seemed to be the only item that had color or seemed to be flourishing. Even the Rev in his somber clothing seemed to fit in at the hospital. The medical staff pointed out the patients with AIDS, because L.A. County backwardly refused to pool its resources to establish an AIDS Ward.[11] When I asked for a vase for my flowers, the attendant seemed bothered and later returned with a plastic urinal. The Rev read the shock on my face and said, "This place needs a lot of things, and one of them is a heart."

The first patient pointed out to us looked like the photographs I had seen of men dying of AIDS. Despite his weakened condition, he lit up when he saw a smiling "man of the cloth" walking toward him. This scene repeated itself often when I accompanied the Rev. Patients never asked if the Rev was Catholic. A man in a collar, hugging them and holding their hand, was much needed medicine for them.

I learned the sick man had been born in Mexico and was two years younger than me. I do not remember his name. Despite being excruciatingly thin, he had plenty of untended thick black hair. His arms had some Kaposi sores, and there was one on his brown face. He smelled like a combination of urine and feces. Close to the end of their lives, these men felt tremendous anxiety regarding their mortality and the afterlife. Because the Rev did not speak Spanish, the patient pulled me close so I could translate for him. I mustered all the energy I had in my body to stay close to him, because inside I felt scared and instinctively wanted to pull away.

As we moved from one Latino patient to another, they voiced similar concerns. Whether in English or in Spanish, it was as if they were repeating a version of the same script. They wanted the Rev to know that they had accepted that they deserved AIDS as a punishment for being gay and having sex. They also felt tremendous shame and guilt for leaving their families behind to pursue their sexual passions. The Rev would assuage those who spoke in English, but he depended on me to translate for those that did not. Some clung to me as they said, "Dile que sé que he pecado y acepto mi castigo." (Tell him that I know I have sinned and accept my punishment.) When I would try to divert the conversation and say, "Stop. It's not like that" in Spanish, they would insist and beg, "¡Dile!" (Tell him!) I followed their directives and repeated their guilt-laden statements about deserving God's wrath. In my personal life, I had spent decades dismissing this type of self-loathing and harmful thinking as falsehoods, but at the request of a dying gay man, I repeated them. Once patients said what they wanted, shed tears, and felt supported, they seemed relieved.

I cannot pinpoint exactly why I returned with the Rev to visit patients with HIV/AIDS. Most of those we visited the previous week were no longer there. I understood that we provided young dying Latino men a moment of kindness—that we allowed them to feel respected, even if what they shared oftentimes disturbed me. I certainly did not think we were saving anyone. After spending my first Friday evening with the Rev at the hospital, I could not wait to get home to take a shower. As I dried off, I felt a wave of guilt for wanting to wash away the stench of AIDS and the memory of the dying young men I encountered that night. I also had the sobering realization that the Rev was right: this disease was on the verge of exploding.

Around the time I accompanied the Rev to the L.A./USC County Hospital, NBC aired the movie *An Early Frost*. The main character was a white gay man who had been diagnosed with AIDS. The movie drew a record number of viewers, and a representative of AIDS Project Los Angeles (APLA) called it "'a very realistic representation of what we know is true in America today.'"[12] The Rev became a much-needed, outspoken advocate for those referred to as "minorities" back in the 1980s. He reminded *L.A. Times* readers of the dangers involved in productions such as *An Early Frost* furthering the perception that AIDS only affected white gay men. Rev Bean warned that more funds needed to be allocated to educating communities of color about HIV/AIDS, and he added, "When people do not think they are in danger of catching [AIDS], they will not take precautions to prevent it."[13]

It would take the Rev a while to reach a semblance of financial security. During its earlier years, the Minority AIDS Project (MAP) relied on volunteers. He wrote in his memoir that "It was 1987, and my finances—as well as MAP's were bleak. I was six months behind in my home rent, ducking the landlord, coming in late and leaving early. They were about to shut off my gas and electricity. I was walking to the office because I couldn't afford a bus pass."[14] Around that time, GLLU helped out and paid a month's rent for MAP, for which the Rev always remained grateful.

Rev Carl Bean was a gospel singer. He had been associated with Motown and even had a minor hit, "I Was Born This Way," in the 1970s. He used his entertainment connections to stage a major fundraiser for MAP in 1988. The singers Dionne Warwick, Patti LaBelle, Natalie Cole, and others donated their time to raise funds for HIV/AIDS awareness. I bought a ticket to "Coming Home for Friends: A Gospel Concert" on August 4, 1988. When I visited the Rev backstage, he introduced me to Dionne. I attended the concert by myself, and as I sat through the show, I came to understand the Rev's strategic brilliance regarding how he was moving forward to anchor his base of support.

The gospel concert was intended to remind African Americans of their collective past—that they had faced challenges before, and now needed to unify for the current one, HIV/AIDS. I realized the Rev knew what he was doing and asked myself, "How can Latinos do something similar?" It was sobering to think that in mid-1988, we could not. The L.A. African American newspaper *The Sentinel* had started reporting about HIV/AIDS in the early 1980s, while Los Angeles's major Spanish-language newspapers had largely ignored the rising infection rate.[15] *La Opinión* waited until later that year to issue a call to action: "With an Open Mind, L.A.'s Latino Community Must Prepare to Battle AIDS." It emphasized the growing number of Latine AIDS cases: "In the first six months of 1988, the number of Latino AIDS cases grew by 35%, the fastest rate of growth among any ethnic group, including whites in the United States."[16] Additionally, the power of the Catholic Church compounded the taboos and stigmas associated with homosexuality in the Latine community. It would never have allowed its members or local churches to affiliate with the open and out Brown queers in GLLU to plan an HIV/AIDS fundraiser.

GLLU had established an AIDS Education Committee in late 1985 to advocate for equitable health policies and more resources for HIV/AIDS education. Oftentimes, more women than men attended the meetings. ACT UP/LA formed in 1987. I cannot overstate how much they influenced all of us and changed the way we organized around HIV/AIDS. Sociologist Benita Roth claims that ACT UP/LA was an "exemplar of progressive, multi-issue, anti-corporate, confrontational movements of the late twentieth century."[17] I attended some of their protests but not their meetings, although I often consulted with and developed a special friendship with Mark Kostopoulos, one of the founders of ACT UP/LA.

In the latter part of 1988, after consulting with long-term GLLU members who pledged their support, I decided to serve as GLLU president. Our collective outrage over the minuscule resources allocated to those with AIDS, the loss of human lives, and the lack of educational information directed to the Spanish-speaking population was undeniable. The death of GLLU members also brought it home. During my first year as GLLU president, everyone joining me on the board of directors was a man. Valentino Sandoval served as vice president and Michael Puente as secretary. A few years later, both died from AIDS.

Immediately after my election, I started planning the anniversary dinner that also represented entering my first year as GLLU president. In a time of soaring HIV/AIDS infections, I wanted to take the Rev's approach of "Coming Home for Friends" and solidify our relationship with the United Farm Workers. Louis Jacinto, who had been raised in Bakersfield and whose family was friends with Dolores Huerta, the cofounder of the UFW, gave me her number. I left a message, and a few days later she called me back. I told her about GLLU, which she said she was familiar with, and asked her to be the keynote speaker at our upcoming anniversary dinner. I specifically asked her to talk about the growing number of HIV/ AIDS cases in the Latine community. She agreed, and I moved forward, including Dolores Huerta on promotional materials.

The GLLU anniversary event was scheduled for October 6, 1988. Unfortunately, three weeks before the event, Huerta, then fifty-eight years old, had suffered broken ribs and lost her spleen due to violence inflicted by the San Francisco police.[18] She was hospitalized for close to a week and eventually recovered, but she could not make it to our GLLU event. At the last minute, I asked attorney Elena Popp, who was active in LU and making a name for herself as a housing advocate, to give the keynote. Despite Dolores Huerta's absence, it turned into a splendid event. Against the advice of the outgoing president, I asked Monica Palacios to perform at the event; after all, I was the new president. Monica's comedy blew everyone away. That night she met Roland Palencia, who had moved on and started VIVA, a group for promoting the creative and artistic talents of Latine queers, and they became fast friends and allies.[19]

I felt tremendous support as GLLU president. Some members who had left returned, and new members were moving in, wanting to take on more responsibility. One of them, Ted Salaises, had joined GLLU a few months before the anniversary celebration. He was twenty-eight years old, four years younger than me. He was meticulously groomed and handsome, and he had great taste in clothes, although he was a bit shy. Ted dove into everything GLLU. He had grown up in Norwalk, a working-class city southeast of Los Angeles, but lived in Silver Lake. When he found out I was from Arizona, Ted shared that he was named after his grandfather, who had been born there. He took on the task of chairing the Social/Cultural Committee and held the meetings at his apartment.

Ted died less than a year later, on October 3, 1989, of AIDS. It happened quickly. One moment we were attending a picnic he planned at Griffith Park, and the next minute he was dead. I was heartbroken. About four of us from GLLU attended his funeral. Ted's family intentionally distanced themselves from us and told others that he had died from a

FIGURE 5.6 1988 GLLU anniversary celebration. Back row, left to right: Oscar, Valentino, David, Michael, author, José, and Irene; front row, left to right: Sandy, Eduardo, Rita, Carla, Veronica, Ted, Eliseo, and Elena. Photograph by Becky Villaseñor.

rare form of cancer. José Hernandez, Oscar de la O, David Trujillo and I consoled each other but made no attempt to approach the family.

During my first year as GLLU president, we decided that we needed to create new HIV/AIDS educational literature ourselves. Service agencies were releasing truly dismal and disappointing prevention and educational literature to inform Spanish-speaking men who were having sex with men about HIV/AIDS. This literature, in addition to its unrealistic portrayals of gay men, lacked cultural sensitivity and ignored the stigma of homosexuality in Latine families. Some pamphlets featured calaveras or skulls that immediately linked HIV/AIDS with death. This connection was intended to reach deep-seated fears and, in turn, encourage abstinence. This was the same logic put forward in 1987 by then-president Ronald Reagan, who I thought of then—and still do now—as the evilest force on the planet. Reagan said he favored educating the public about

HIV/AIDs through "values of right and wrong" and promoting abstinence.[20] I favored education efforts that provided information about safe
sex for gay men and encouraged the use of condoms.

The AIDS Education Committee spearheaded and collectively wrote
the text for a pamphlet that we titled "Dios, usted y el SIDA" (God, You
and AIDS). I am sure my visits to L.A./USC General County Hospital
with the Rev greatly influenced the pamphlet's overall message. It attempted to dispel the myth that AIDS was a punishment, and it offered
a sex-positive message to Brown monolingual Spanish-speaking men
engaging in sex with other men. It emphasized that HIV/AIDS was a
preventable disease and advocated the use of condoms. We did not use
the word gay on the cover; instead, we put forth an image that Brown
men could identify with. After much persuading, Valentino Sandoval
and Ernesto Borges Torres, both active in the AIDS Education Committee, agreed to have their faces on the pamphlet.

I choreographed the photoshoot at Valentino's apartment in Hollywood, and Louis Jacinto, GLLU's resident photographer, brought his
camera and other equipment. The shoot was laden with distractions.
Valentino said, "I don't want to look fey." "But you are fey!" Louis remarked. I added to the unruliness by asking, "What's fey?" A debate
ensued leading me to deduce that they did not want to look too flamboyant or effeminate. I positioned their bodies and moved Valentino's arms
around Ernesto. I gently coaxed them often, "Nobody's going to think
you two are a couple," and, "You know we gotta do this." I learned a lot
of inside information about gay men's posturing and humor that night,
and I commend Louis for capturing such a powerful shot. We started
distributing the pamphlet in the spring of 1989. Unfortunately, I did not
keep a copy of it, probably because they were so much in demand. We
were overwhelmed with requests from New York City, Chicago, Mexico,
and other Latin American countries, and less than a year later, we printed
another 5,000 copies.[21]

As a grassroots organization, GLLU never sought to create a new
AIDS agency. Initially, we moved to confront HIV/AIDS by working
in partnership with other groups to disseminate information regarding
prevention and to advocate for health services, but the mounting num-

FIGURE 5.7 Valentino Sandoval and Ernesto Borges Torres, 1988. Photograph by Louis Jacinto.

ber of gay Latinos acquiring HIV pressed us to start our own HIV/AIDS agency. In July 1989 GLLU formally voted to launch Bienestar: A Gay Latino AIDS Project. Also in July, after intense lobbying and pressure, the Centers for Disease Control (CDC) provided GLLU's Bienestar its first public funding, in the amount of $30,000, and I formed a GLLU AIDS Advisory Board to help inform and advise me and the board of directors.[22] We opened a separate account for our new agency, to ensure more reliable accounting for the incoming funds, but despite the advisors, GLLU's board of directors controlled every aspect of Bienestar.

We secured an office in a perfect location, at 3938 Sunset Boulevard, right underneath the Sunset Junction sign near Sanborn Avenue. We paid $512.00 a month in rent. I also wrote a grant to get computers for the office. GLLU finally had an office to hold its committee and board meetings in. I was beaming at our Bienestar open house until someone from APLA approached me and remarked, "This is the office? It is so small, I expected something much bigger." The comment stung, but for the first time in its history, GLLU had its own space and held the keys to a building.

Unfortunately, the GLLU Board and I hired our first executive director only to let him go after three months, because the CDC funds did not arrive until early the next year. Bienestar ended up $10,000 in debt. Luckily, the AIDS Healthcare Foundation loaned us the money to keep our newly launched AIDS project going.

Despite the fiscal challenges, I felt that we were on the right course and that we needed to keep moving forward with Bienestar. The GLLU membership agreed and elected me to serve another year as GLLU president. Because we were moving into a new arena that involved contract obligations and funding, the GLLU board was expanded to include more positions. I also insisted that they take turns chairing the large meetings to boost their confidence and agree to serve as GLLU officers in the future. Luckily, late in 1989, the U.S. Conference of Mayors committed $50,000 to Bienestar to organize a series of AIDS seminars in Spanish in the Los Angeles area.

In addition to an open house, GLLU held a Kick-Off Party for Bienestar at the Jewel's Catch-One on February 18, 1990. As we did for most of our major fundraising events, we contracted Claudette the Sexy D.J., catered a buffet, and sold tickets in advance. The event was a success, and I gave a speech from the stage of the Catch One that night. I looked down and saw in the audience below many notable queer activists, such as Ivy Bottini and the venerated Jewel Thais-Williams, listening to and clapping for me. In that moment, I realized I had become everything I once dreamed of being: I had become the person who spoke out for Brown queer rights.

My mind darted off again as I walked off the stage. I looked across the large night club and caught a flicker of my younger self. I could see myself dancing and floating across the Catch's pulsating, crowded dance floor relishing my sense of autonomy and freedom. I had much to celebrate that

FIGURE 5.8   GLLU Board of Directors in 1989 at Bienestar office. Back row, left to right: Dana (Public Relations), author (President), Tomas (Vice President), Irene (Special Projects), Oscar (Treasurer); front row, left to right: Juan (Public Relations), Ron (Recording Secretary) and Louis (membership Director). Pat Martel (Programs Administrator) is missing. Courtesy of Louis Jacinto Collection.

night, but I was exhausted when I reached my apartment. It occurred to me that except for fundraising events, I never went to the Catch to enjoy the music and dance. Going to the movies on Saturday afternoons had also fallen by the wayside. My life had become one of rushing from one meeting to the next. Somehow, my time had become regulated. It needed to be dedicated to the collective good, and not to myself.

Later that month, after the Catch-One event, the National Commission on AIDS invited me to testify at their Los Angeles hearing. I considered it an honor. I went over my remarks with the GLLU board and spoke from the heart. I mentioned that Bienestar was the only openly gay Latino AIDS project in California, and I reminded the commissioners that most people with AIDS in Latine communities were gay and bisexual and, "if the money was distributed according to this [aspect]. . . . I would be sitting here before you representing the largest Latino AIDS agency in the city, in this county, [but] unfortunately it's just the oppo-

FIGURE 5.9 Author speaking at the Catch One, 1990. Photograph by Louis Jacinto.

site." I also reminded the commission that Latinos "get lost in translation" and "that homophobia is killing us."[23]

While the commissioners were in Los Angeles, a group called the Latino Community Leadership, with a history of serving the straight community, invited the commissioners to a trendy restaurant in East Los Angeles. They invited a few Latine queers as an afterthought, and the meeting turned contentious. All of the active representatives at the meeting were employed in the AIDS work sector. While advocacy was written into their job descriptions, I needed to take off work to attend the luncheon. I was also increasingly finding myself outside the networks that met weekly to discuss potential HIV/AIDS funding and collaborations.

By the end of 1990, I had completed my second year as GLLU president. I felt accomplished. Bienestar: A Gay Latino AIDS Project continued to grow and move forward, and it was no longer in debt. But despite the success, I was becoming less adept at juggling the various aspects

FIGURE 5.10   Author and Oscar de la O after National Commission on AIDS testimony, 1990. Photograph by Louis Jacinto,

of my activism, which had become my life. The mounting deaths from AIDS also sometimes made it hard for me to appreciate how my activism had made a difference.

At 35 years old, it also seemed like everyone around me had moved into careers where they could advocate for queer rights in one form or another and earned a living from it. New HIV/AIDS agencies were forming, and established ones were digging in their heels despite their ineffectiveness. The jostling for funding was intense. It was distressing to witness and harder to avoid getting caught in the crossfire. Despite fulfillment as an electrician, my body was also sending me signals that became difficult to ignore. The stiffness in my knees in the mornings took longer to wear off. By the end of 1990, as I considered my future, and the path that lay before me, it no longer included GLLU or working in construction.

Conclusion

A s 1991 greeted me, I immersed myself in Anne Rice's vampire novels and started spending my entire Sundays at Venice Beach. I became close friends with the new Gay and Lesbian Latinos Unidos (GLLU) president, Tomas Soto, who had served as vice president during my second term. A few former members who had served with me on the board of directors also returned, and I sincerely felt they were prepared to move GLLU—particularly Bienestar—forward. In many ways, leaving allowed them the room to blossom and take fuller control. I have never regretted the decision. I needed to create a new path.

Before I left GLLU entirely, I directed one last major fundraiser. The profits were divided equally between Bienestar and the Latina Lesbian Support Group in East Los Angeles. I booked El Vez for a Cinco de Mayo fundraiser. Although he preferred to be known as a translator instead of an Elvis impersonator, "The Mexican Elvis" was known for performing "You Ain't Nothin' but a Chihuahua" and "Está Bien, Mamacita."[1] I booked what I considered the coolest of L.A. places, the elegant Union Station Restaurant, which was empty at the time and rented out for events. The restaurant was built before World War II, and its brass windows, balcony, high decorative ceilings, and hanging chandeliers made me feel like I had stepped back in time. We offered a no-host bar where Andy Lopez, who always did the centerpieces for the GLLU anniversary dinners, served his Andy "Con Ganas" Margaritas. We made it happen and raised $2,000. When I walked away from the event, I felt like I had staged my own going away party.

As I pondered my future, I did not feel pulled toward any profession. I preferred to stay away from the AIDS and social services sectors. A

GAY AND LESBIAN LATINOS UNIDOS

INVITES YOU TO A

Cinco de Mayo

Fiesta

Kicking off our 10th Anniversary !

Saturday, May 4th 1991   6 PM to Midnight

at the Landmark **Union   Station   Restaurant**
800 N. Alameda St., Los Angeles

with a special performance   by

El Vez

"The Mexican Elvis"
with Priscillita and
Que Linda Thompson

Strolling   Mariachis
Dancing to **Claudette, "The Sexy DJ"**
Antojitos and No Host Bar   Featuring Andy's "Con Ganas" Margaritas
and a Midnight Raffle of a Cruise for Two along the   Mexican Riviera

$20

($25 after April 27)
Raffle tickets - $5

Tickets available at a Different Light Bookstore, 4013 and 8853 Santa Monica Blvd.
and at BIENESTAR, 3938 Sunset Boulevard (at Sanborn), Los Angeles, California
Cruise courtesy of **Coordinated Travel Management Inc.** (213) 652-9222

GLLU A benefit for Gay and Lesbian Latinos Unidos   including
BIENESTAR: A Gay Latino AIDS Project
years and the Latina Lesbian Support Groups

For   More   Information   Call   (213) 660-9681

FIGURE C.1 Poster created by author, 1991. Private collection of author.

nagging voice in my head would not allow me to forget that I had failed to get a bachelor's degree despite attending college for four years. I also recognized that completing my degree would provide new career options, so I enrolled in evening classes at California State University in L.A. (Cal State L.A.). I began by taking two evening courses while still working as an electrician to support myself. Sometimes I took time off from work to expedite my studies. In 1992, I earned a bachelor's degree in social sciences, an interdisciplinary degree that allowed me to take several enriching Geography, History, and Chicane courses that provided critical theories that helped me name and informed my understanding of what I had witnessed during my lifetime.

I had taken a few courses with the feminist historian Dr. Carole Srole, who encouraged me to apply to the master's program in History and generously volunteered to serve as my advisor. I had never considered a graduate degree, but I had thoroughly enjoyed my experiences at Cal State L.A. and my courses. Cal State L.A. prioritized working students like me and held their graduate classes in the evenings. Flattered and intrigued, I applied and was accepted into the master's program, but I continued to support myself as an electrician. In fact, I worked at some of my most memorable jobs in the early 1990s, including laying the underground electrical wiring to power the future Universal CityWalk.

The Universal CityWalk job required me to jump in and out of ditches to lay 4-inch conduit to carry power to all the stores, restaurants, and activities in the large entertainment promenade. The job required working more as a team with the other electricians. Once Universal Studios opened in the morning, the audio of all their shows in the distance blared throughout our work area. Miami Vice was the closest and loudest, and we timed and mimicked the explosions.

Once, our foreman sent me to meet one of the studio technicians to figure out why the mechanical King Kong, a part of the Universal Studio tour, had frozen. I walked through the park with my toolbelt on my shoulder, not having a clue what was expected of me. When I reached the attraction, I admired the large but stationary gorilla and the replica New York City buildings while I waited. I had ridden the tram through the attraction a few times and knew the premise of the ride was that

King Kong managed to get loose and intended to destroy the city and the Brooklyn Bridge. For the finale, the gorilla grabbed the tram full of people and brought them close to his face to frighten them. It was one of my favorite rides at Universal Studios. I felt like the luckiest person in the world.

A technician approached me and said, "Oh, you are perfect." It turned out that he needed me to climb inside King Kong to check the components and wiring inside. I was five-foot four, and able to fit through the constricted area in the gorilla's interior. He opened a door behind King Kong and instructed me to climb the ladder, then hop onto another ladder inside the body until I could see out through the gorilla's mouth. He gave me a flashlight and showed me how to work the walkie talkie, and I strapped both across my shoulders. I could not wait to get inside. I climbed the thin metal ladders carefully and steered clear of all the cables. When I reached the mouth, the technician told me where to find the controls and how to reset them. I crawled out before the mechanical creature started to move, and the technician let me hang out while he tested the ride a few times. I took my time walking through the theme park to rejoin my crew. I even stopped and bought a Coke. When I returned, I bragged, "They needed me to fix King Kong!" They were jealous they were not chosen and wanted to know all the details.

Once I became a journeyperson, I encountered more hostile behavior on worksites because of my queerness. I no longer worked under a male partner or coworker, and oftentimes I worked alone. I also earned more money than most of the other workers on the job sites. The hostile acts came not from fellow electricians but from men in the other trades. A painter once decided to follow me and painted "dyke" on the walls where I was working.

One hot afternoon, a muscular, white iron worker fainted and made a loud noise when he fell. I went over to check out what happened, and so did everyone else nearby. Someone poured some water on him, and he regained consciousness. If I had fainted, it would have been treated as comical and expected. Since an iron worker fainted, the job's construction superintendent considered the heat a serious matter, called it a day, and sent us all home with pay. The next week, the iron worker decided to play a "joke" on me. Typically, when I went to get supplies or on break, I would take off my tool belt and drop it where I was working, and it would remain untouched until I returned. This day, I found my tool belt had been emptied and my tools scattered around. The iron worker and his friends laughed and pointed at me as I collected my items. The electrical foreman came over and reprimanded them for "horsing around" and holding up work, and I heard the iron worker say, "Who cares about that dyke. She is taking a job from a man with children."

A week later, in November 1991, I came back from lunch and the man that had fainted and two other white iron workers were bent over in tears. I had never seen men bawling so openly. I walked over to a Latino laborer and asked what happened. He told me that Magic Johnson from the L.A. Lakers had just announced he had AIDS. I watched the homophobic men in disbelief as they openly grieved the beloved NBA superstar's diagnosis.

I reminded myself that I made more money than the men who directed their hatred toward me. Even so, it touched a deep place. The incidents reminded me of when I was a child and experienced acts of racism with my mother, such as not being attended to in stores. She advised me not to say anything, because "Our money is just as good as theirs." Perhaps I am guilty of resorting to the same defense mechanisms decades later. When I tell people that I was a construction worker, they tend to overglamorize my role. Although these types of incidents were rare, they did happen, and they served to remind me of the simmering hate some people had for me.

On the home front, during the early 1990s I actively dated and entered a serious relationship. On April 29, 1992, I was dating Rosie, a woman with two teenage children, when the Rodney King uprisings started. I had just finished walking the Griffith Park Observatory Trail. As I drove toward my house, the K-LOVE radio announcer interrupted Rocío Dúrcal singing one of my favorite songs, "Costumbres," to warn listeners to stay away from Florence and Normandy avenues in South Los Angeles. He warned that violence had erupted in response to the not-guilty verdicts handed out to the police officers who had been caught on camera pummeling Rodney King. At first, the events that unfolded seemed distant, but in less than two days, they reached my neighborhood, near Vermont Avenue and Santa Monica Boulevard. Rosie called me to ask that I pick up her children because their schools had been forced to close. It was hard to explain what was happening to her children, because I did not fully understand it either. Rosie lived in the hilly area of Silver Lake, and I stayed at her house because it was further away from the uprisings. I often walked to an empty lot across the street from Rosie's house to look at the smoke and fires in the distance. Like most people, I found it hard to believe that so much of Los Angeles was on fire.

When I returned to my apartment, empty shoe boxes from Payless Shoes were adrift everywhere on the streets. Despite the imposed curfew, I drove around in the early mornings to survey the damage and to witness a type of destruction I never thought I would witness. The roads were relatively empty and armored tanks rolled down the streets, but no one tried to stop me. The immediacy and effectiveness of Los Angeles's clean-up efforts surprised me, considering the damage I witnessed.

Rosie and I did not last long. She worked at an AIDS agency and had asked a mutual friend to introduce us. As a side job, she sang at a club in Hollywood, Faces, on Sunday nights. As soon as we started dating, she insisted that I accompany her there. The crowd was mostly Spanish-speaking Latinas who adhered strongly to butch and femme roles. Rosie knew I needed training in bar etiquette before my first visit to Faces. She told me that she did not want to dance with anyone and that I needed to be possessive. She instructed me, "When butch women ask you if they can dance with me, say 'no.'" "Why would anyone ask me permission to dance with you? Why don't they ask you?" I responded. I knew the pattern, but I wanted to point out that it made me uncomfortable to speak for her in that way. "Because that's how it's done," she said. Sure enough, a few women asked me if they could dance with Rosie and I said, "No. I think she's tired." One butch retorted, "She doesn't look tired to me," turned, and asked Rosie if she was tired, but she did not break protocol by directly asking Rosie to dance.

Rosie had a problem with my reply and further instructed me that, "When women ask you to dance with me just say 'no.' Be a butch." That request raised all sorts of red flags. The butches I said no to glared at me the rest of the night and were sometimes combative. No surprise that my relationship with Rosie did not last long. I started finding excuses not to go to Faces, especially because I often had homework and reading to do. Rosie had no problem finding a more willing protector to take my place.

Around 1993, I met a Chicana raised in East Los Angeles who I thought was the woman of my dreams. Her nickname was Pony. She was seven years younger than me, taught second grade, and loved dancing and the Dodgers. A few years before we met, Henry, a gay Latino she partied with, had invited her to a GLLU fundraiser. When they arrived, Henry told her, "See those women over there? They are the Lesbianas Unidas. Stay away from them. They are radicals." He pointed me out and said, "See that one. Make sure you stay away from that one because she is the worst of the bunch." Henry's reaction was not rare. Many considered us too political, outspoken, and radical. Pony remembered me, and when we were at the same house party years later, she made it a point to flirt and introduce herself. We entered a relationship and lived together for a number of years. We had great times, but the seven-year age difference caused problems. Pony had too many expectations of me, and I often felt like Pony's parent, which always kills a relationship. Nevertheless, Pony was there for me when I faced a major health crisis.

In 1994, the Northridge earthquake caused devastating damage to the L.A. Memorial Coliseum.[2] I was part of the construction crew working 10-hour days, seven days a week to get the stadium ready before the beginning of the football season in September. Both the University of Southern California and the L.A. Raiders used the stadium. On June 25, I suffered a severe job-related injury. A worker on a scaffold above me dropped a sandblaster just as I was walking beneath him. It landed on my head. My hard hat lessened the impact, but it knocked me to the ground. I did not lose consciousness, but I was disoriented. A coworker helped get me on my feet, walked me through a tunnel to get outside, and sat me in one of the stadium seats while I tried to get my bearings.

The impact jammed my hard hat down on my head, and blood trickled down the right side of my face. My coworker helped me pull off the hard hat and yanked a pencil out of my scalp. I had tucked it behind my right ear, and it had penetrated and scratched my skull during the accident, causing the bleeding. When I asked him what happened, he said, "A sandblaster fell on your head." I knew then that my days as a blue-collar tradesperson were over.

In the last few years, I had found it increasingly difficult to keep up physically with being an electrician. As I sat there in the historic stadium, looking at the football field while more workers gathered around me to find out what had happened, I realized I had waited too long to make my next move. There is nothing more direct than a chingaso, or a blow to the head, to make a point.

I was plagued with vertigo for about six months after the accident. It caused permanent damage to my neck and other residual nerve damage. To this day I have restricted movement in both hands, especially in my thumbs. Not being able to earn a living as an electrician meant making big changes in my life. Unbeknownst to me, I had already planted the seeds that would result in an unusual career transformation, from blue-collar worker to scholar. Not that one profession is better than the other, but higher education placed less strenuous demands on my body. I was in the early years of my master's program when I suffered the injury, and because I was in a labor union, they financially supported my rehabilitation and paid the tuition costs involved in completing my program.

In 1996, when I completed my master's degree, Dr. Srole learned that a history professor at Santa Monica College needed to go on emergency leave. She recommended me to fill the open position. I also taught a few classes in Chicane Studies at Cal State Los Angeles. The opportunity gave me a glimpse of what being a professor entailed, and I found myself enjoying this new chapter in my life.

The next year, on my visits to Tucson, I noticed that my mother was having more difficulty taking care of herself. In the past she would prepare a huge pot of cocido (Mexican beef soup) to celebrate my arrival in Tucson. On recent visits, however, she would say, "Oh! What a great surprise," even though I had informed her of my plans during my weekly phone calls. Her grooming had declined noticeably, and when I took her to the grocery store, she loaded her cart with mostly cookies and cinnamon rolls. I usually slept on the living room couch during my visits. After she went to bed in her room, I continued to watch television, but she started returning to the living room to say, "I forgot you were here and I thought I left the TV on." It was troubling for me to witness her decline, but I got to leave and return to the safety of my life in Los Angeles.

I never thought I would consider returning to Tucson, but my mother needed help, Pony and I were over, and waiting was not an option. I knew that finding a job in Tucson was close to impossible and that my physical disabilities would restrict my employment prospects. Completing the PhD program in History at the University of Arizona seemed like the only viable option. I entered the program in 1998 and lived in the house I grew up in with my mother while I attended classes. Even when I moved all my things back to my childhood home, I had every intention of returning to Los Angeles. My mother died in 2002, a year before I received my doctorate. I never applied to teaching positions in Los Angeles, because by then, housing costs had started to rise—and I received an offer in my hometown that was too good to pass up: I became a professor at the University of Arizona in Tucson. I have lived in Tucson ever since.

TUCSON, ARIZONA, MARCH 2023

I always knew that one of Laura Aguilar's photographs of me would grace the cover of this memoir, but I assumed it would be the one of me holding the guitar. When I saw the photograph of me with the freeway behind me, I knew it would make the perfect cover. I last connected with Laura Aguilar in 2004. I had some large 16×20 framed portraits that ended up in my possession. One of them was of Susana Brito, who had moved to Florida and entrusted her portrait to me to return to Laura. On one of my trips to Los Angeles, I packed the portraits into my car and made a date to meet Laura for lunch.

Laura had a generous spirit. She wanted her friends to enjoy her art, and she did not seek to profit in the exchange. Printing out the large photographs was time consuming and costly, as was framing them. During our meal, Laura shared that she had spent time in San Antonio and had even been to England. As she collected the portraits I was returning, she said, "I had forgotten about these. You could have kept them." "Laura," I replied, "These are beautiful, but they belong to you." She gave me her mischievous smile, and we promised to stay in touch but never did. Laura Aguilar died in 2018.[3]

I also lost touch with Reverend Bean when I moved. He went on to become an archbishop and died in 2021.[4] The L.A. City Council designated the intersection of Jefferson Boulevard and Sycamore Avenue in South Los Angeles as "Archbishop Carl Bean Square." Pop icon Lady Gaga recorded a version of his 1970s Motown song "I Was Born This Way" in 2011, and it is now known by many as the "Gay Pride Anthem." Interestingly, the former L.A./USC General Hospital building where we visited Latines with AIDS is currently being converted into affordable housing units.[5]

Although it faced a bumpy start, Bienestar continued to grow and expand. It separated from GLLU in 1994 and formed its own board of directors. Oscar de la O, a veteran GLLU member who served as treasurer when I was president, took over as Bienestar's executive director. Rita Gonzáles, a longtime Radio GLLU host, has also been a consistent presence; she has served on the Bienestar board since 1994. Today, Bienestar Human Services operates a number of centers that provide full-service medical care, HIV/AIDS treatment and prevention, sexual health, mental health, substance use counseling, and medication-assisted treatment. It continues to focus on identifying and addressing emerging health issues faced by the Latine and LGBTQIA+ populations.[6]

Tensions between Lesbianas Unidas and GLLU also forced a separation in 1994. I had left three years earlier, but gauging from the telephone calls I received back then, I believe the separation was not as amicable as some would like us to think. Although both groups continued to meet, they became less active and slowly became dormant—until recently. In late 2021, Roland Palencia called me to tell me about a new documentary about GLLU he was producing and wanted me to be part of. I remained a bit skeptical until the film crew and about eight former GLLU members met on a Zoom call. Once we started talking about the past, it seemed like old times again.

A COVID spike the last few months of 2021 caused me to miss the reunion captured at the documentary's conclusion. Filmmaker Gregorio Davila drove to Tucson to interview me on camera in February 2022. My thyroid medication had suddenly stopped working, and I felt fatigued and nervous during the interview. Gregorio tried his best to put me at ease, and I discovered the depth of his kindheartedness. I agreed to respond to questions about my time in GLLU, but as I was one of eight people profiled, I recognize that I am only one perspective out of many.

I had an opportunity to preview the documentary, but I turned it down, because I wanted to trust the process and the creative people involved. I attended the premier of *Unidad: Gay and Lesbian Latinos Unidos* on June 3, 2022. It was good to connect with everyone, and I loved what I thought was the final product. In 2023, however, PBS became involved. They requested the documentary be reworked and lengthened for television. As of this writing, I have not seen the revised documentary, but I trust it will bring attention to GLLU and its accomplishments. Sadly, Geneva Fernández passed away shortly after the premier and we will all miss sharing future events and conversations with her once it goes into national distribution and reaches larger audiences.

In late 2022, the ONE Archives Foundation curated an exhibition called "Together on the Air" that chronicled Radio GLLU's legacy from its inception in 1986 through the 1990s.[7] The ONE Archives claimed that Radio GLLU was "the first bilingual LGBTQIA+ radio program in the country." Because I was one of the original voices on Radio GLLU, the ONE Archives Foundation invited me to take part in their exhibition's opening and closing, which allowed me to meet some dedicated content creators and queer archivists of color. I found their interest in preserving and showcasing history refreshing and exciting.

As I mentioned in the introduction, each time I moved in Los Angeles, I prioritized and protected the contents of a box where I squirreled away photographs of events and the Brown queer activists I worked alongside. That year, my essay, "My Archive: 20 Years of Los Angeles' LGBTQ+ Movement" appeared in *High Country News*, where I related the importance of the items I had collected over the years.[8] I had often considered donating them to an archive, and this essay prompted a few

L.A.
A *QUEER* HISTORY & FILM BLISS STUDIOS

PRESENT

WORLD PREMIERE SCREENING

UNIDAD

GAY & LESBIAN LATINOS UNIDOS

A SHORT DOCUMENTARY FILM

Directed by GREGORIO DAVILA

Executive PRODUCER ROLAND PALENCIA

Producer MARIO J. NOVOA

Featuring Photos by LOUIS JACINTO

Friday, June 3, 2022 - Renberg Theater, Hollywood, CA

FIGURE C.2 *Unidad* Premier Handout, 2022. Private collection of author.

archives, all in the Los Angeles area, to express interest in my collection. As I put the finishing touches on *L.A. Interchanges*, I recognized that I no longer needed the primary documents in my possession. Since I am 68 years old, finding a permanent place for them ranked high on my to-do list. I fervently believed they should be housed in an institution that will appreciate them and make them available to the public.

A few months ago, Ani Boyadjian, research and special collections manager at the L.A. Central Library, arranged for me to meet with her and three other archivists. They had prepared some mock displays and information about future cataloging for my collection. Each of the archivists also expressed what my donation would mean to them and the library. I was impressed by their presentation, and I felt extremely appreciated. I agreed to donate my materials to the L.A. Central Library.

I walked away with a "swag bag" full of L.A. Public Library goodies and the knowledge that my collection would be moving into a good home. Every item included in *L.A. Interchanges* and in my collection will eventually be available to the public and to future researchers. My collection will also be stored alongside former GLLU member Louis Jacinto's collection of photographs, many of which are featured in this book. The Irene Martínez and Laura Duran Collection, which I think represents the largest collection of LU and East L.A. Support Group materials, will also be housed at the L.A. Central Library.

L.A. Interchanges only touched the surface of the histories that need to be told about Latine organizing in the 1980s. It, the *Unidad* documentary, and exhibits such as the one on Radio GLLU will bring attention to GLLU and will hopefully inspire interest in queer history. In recent conversations I have had with young queers, they seem to always express a strong interest in learning more about their past. Doing so serves as a means of empowerment for them. I feel like my efforts have pushed that inspiration and learning forward.

Endings are always hard, but this one feels like a victory. I will always love Los Angeles. As much as a city is able to, I feel like it embraced and nourished me. When I moved there in 1978, I considered it a place of possibility. It fulfilled my expectations and more.

NOTES

INTRODUCTION

1. Alice Y. Hom interviewed over 50 lesbian activists of color for her dissertation. Many are available at the UCLA Chicano Studies Research Center; see "Unifying Differences: Lesbian of Color Community Building in Los Angeles and New York, 1970s–1980s," PhD diss., Claremont Graduate University, 2011.

2. In *Baby, You Are My Religion: Women, Gay Bars, and Theology* (London and New York: Routledge Press, 2014), Marie Carter writes about the importance of mostly pre-Stonewall bars to lesbian identity, lesbian partnerships, and their sense of being a part of something bigger. She interviewed a sizable number of lesbians of different generations and claims that to many, "a bar [was] more than a bar"; instead, they were spaces of community building with similar attachments as "an actual church." See page 3.

3. In addition to primary sources, the historian in me remains profoundly dedicated to the footnote and intends to include a few as a means to inform future scholars seeking to write inclusive histories. I also include materials from archives and newspaper articles when needed to ensure a more precise timeline and to strengthen the connection to the past. Additional primary documents are also available in the Appendix.

4. If I had written this book last year, I would have used *Latinx* as a gender-inclusive collective term of identity. But as I discuss often throughout the chapters that follow with regard to my own ethnic and especially my gender identity—identities shift, change, and evolve. Thus, I have decided to use *Latine*.

CHAPTER 1

1. George J. Sánchez, *Boyle Heights: How a Los Angeles Neighborhood Became the Future of American Democracy* (University of California Press, 2021), 5.

2. I dissect and offer more details about my relationship with my mother, family history and coming of age as a queer child in my previous book, *In the Shadows of the Freeway: Growing Up Brown & Queer* (Tucson, Arizona: Planet Earth Press, 2019).

3. Valverde was born in 1932 and arrested for the first time in 1948 at the age of 17. For more information, see the documentary *Nancy from Eastside Clover*, directed by Gregorio Davila (Los Angeles: Film Bliss Studios, 2014). Also see Shmuel Gonzales, "Nancy From Eastside Clover, Lincoln Heights (Queer History)," *Barrio Boychick: Your Latino-Jewish Friend in the Los Angeles Eastside*, June 30, 2017, https://barrioboychik.com/2017/06/30/nancy-from -eastside-clover-lincoln-heights-queer-history-ela/, accessed April 9, 2022.

4. See Kath Weston, "Get Thee to a Big City: Sexual Imaginary and the Great Gay Migration," *GLQ* 2, no. 3 (June 1, 1995): 253–277. Weston notes that this LGTBQ+ migration trend continued but at a less "furious pace" than in the 1970s and early 1980s.

5. National Gay Task Force, *Our Right to Love: A Lesbian Resource Book*, ed. Ginny Vida (Englewood Cliffs, New Jersey: Prentice-Hall, 1978), 249.

6. The issue released close to the time I moved to LA stressed self-defense and reminded readers to be aware of the dangers posed by the Hillside Strangler who had raped and murdered 13 women in the LA area. Sharon McDonald, "A Matter of Rape and Death," page 6–7 in *The Lesbian Tide: A Feminist Lesbian Publication, Written by and for the Rising Tide of Women Today* (hereafter *Tide*), January/February 1978.

7. Ernest Holsendolph, "U.S. Moves to Require Contractors to Hire Women on Federal Jobs," *New York Times*, August 11, 1977, page 39.

CHAPTER 2

1. Early-20th-century boosters in Hollywood decided to exploit the nation's infatuation with Egyptian culture and built a movie theater to anchor future commercial development. According to Bruce Handy, "And Not Just Any Movie Theater: It Would Be One of the Most Spectacular the World Had Ever Seen." See "Watch Like an Egyptian," *Vanity Fair*, January 29, 2008, https://www.vanityfair.com/news/2008/01/egyptomania200801.

2. Karen Tongson is correct about my generation's fascination with drummer and singer Karen Carpenter. See *Why Karen Carpenter Matters* (Austin, Texas: University of Texas Press, 2019).

3. Joan is a pseudonym, as is Henry. These are the only names in this book that I have changed because I wish to respect their privacy and do not want to out Joan or discuss her queer past without her consent.

4. Monica Palacios, "That Time Melissa Ethridge Gave Me 5 Minutes," Lesbian Game Changers, October 5, 2016. At https://www.lesbiangcemag.com /2021/10/that-time-melissa-etheridge-gave-me-5-mins/, accessed March 12, 2023.

5. Steve Rose makes a similar observation in "Teddy Pendergrass: Sex, Drugs and the Tragic Life of the 'Black Elvis'" (*The Guardian*, March 2, 2019), https://www.theguardian.com/culture/2019/mar/02/teddy-pendergrass-if -you-dont-know-me-sex-drugs-and-the-tragic-life-of-the-black-elvis, accessed December 30, 2022.

6. The first pride parade took place in 1970 and the original route ran along Hollywood Boulevard, see "Christopher Street West / L.A. Pride Parade" Los Angeles Conservancy at https://www.laconservancy.org/locations /christopher-street-west-la-pride-parade, accessed February 13, 2023.

7. An announcement of the LA Pride Parade can be found in the *Tide*, July–August 1979, page 29. Interestingly, Los Angeles Deputy Mayor Grace Montañez Davis, a Mexican American born in LA's Lincoln Heights, was the parade's grand marshal that year. Mayor Thomas (Tom) Bradley appointed Montañez Davis, who is recognized as one of the founders of the Mexican American Political Association and the Chicana feminist group Comisión Feminil Mexicana, as deputy mayor. For more information, see Vicki Ruíz and Virginia Sánchez Korrol, *Latinas in the United States: A Historical Encyclopedia* (Bloomington: Indiana University Press, 2006), 187–188.

8. The two-page "The National Lesbian Feminist Organization" handout indicates the NFLO's strong efforts to recruit and include more lesbians of color. This outreach announcement is signed by Susan Rodriguez of Oakland, California. In ONE Institute, Lesbians of Color-Los Angeles File.

9. Flying Clouds wrote a letter to the feminist newspaper *off our backs* that praised LOC. See Flying Clouds, "Speaking to the Heart," *off our backs* 9, no. 6, "AIN'T I A WOMON?" (June 1979), p. 26. As Flying Clouds made clear in this letter, she had already left Los Angeles and LOC when her letter was published. By the time I started attending LOC meetings, most of the women who established or founded LOC, such as Flying Clouds and da da, had moved on.

10. Randy Shilts provides the most comprehensive insight into this matter in *Conduct Unbecoming: Lesbians and Gays in the U.S. Military* (New York: St. Martin's Press, 1994). This article notes that Lesbians of Color supported this rally, "Navy Discharged Six Sailors because of Lesbian Activity," *Times-Advocate* (Escondido, California), June 15, 1980, p. 3.

11. Thanks to Irene Martínez, Emma Pérez, and Robin Podolsky, who shared some insights from the protest with me. All three attended the protest on Santa Monica Boulevard that cold December night.

12. "Lesbians of Color Picket Palms," *Lesbian News*, February 1980. In ONE Institute, Lesbians of Color-Los Angeles File.

13. Noelle Carter, "Historic Lesbian Bar The Palms Set to Close in West Hollywood." May 8, 2013 at https://www.latimes.com/food/dailydish/la-dd-historic -lesbian-bar-the-palms-set-to-close-in-west-hollywood-20130507-story .html, accessed December 22, 2022.

14. Elizabeth Mehren, "L.A. Image: Rape Capital," *Los Angeles Times* (hereafter *L.A. Times*), April 18, 1980, p. 62.

15. David Shaw, "Media Failed to Examine Alleged LAPD Abuses :Press: Eulia Love Case Brought a Tougher Look. But Complaints About Patterns of Use of Force Weren't Explored," *L.A. Times*, May 26, 1992, Page 1.

16. A documentary about the Catch was released in 2018. See August Brown, "The Story of L.A. Club Jewel's Catch One and Its Pioneering Owner Finds Its Way to Netflix," *L.A. Times*, May 2, 2018, at https://www.latimes.com /entertainment/music/la-et-ms-jewels-catch-one-documentary-20180502 -story.html, accessed January 3, 2023.

CHAPTER 3

1. I understand the concept of performativity in queer studies but identifying as butch back then and now still feels like a pretense.

2. Jeanne Cordova, "Are Roles Really Dead?" *Tide*, July/August 1979, page 5–6.

3. Ibid., page 6.

4. I discuss this episode of Tucson history in my first book, *La Calle: Spatial Conflicts and Urban Renewal in a Southwest City* (Tucson: University of Arizona Press, 2010).

5. Geographer Wendy Cheng attributes the ethnic shifts I witnessed to global economic restructuring. See *The Changs Next Door to the Díazes: Remapping Race in Suburban California* (Minneapolis: University of Minnesota Press, 2013), 5–8.

6. Yolanda Retter Vargas died in 2007. See Elaine Woo, "Yolanda Retter; Controversial Activist for Lesbian, Minority Rights," *L.A. Times*, August 29, 2007, page 23. In addition to other writings, in 1999, Retter wrote a dissertation "On the Side of Angels: Lesbian Activism in Los Angeles" (University of New Mexico). Confirming that it is indeed a small world, former La Las member Emma Pérez served as a member of Yolanda's dissertation committee.

7. In 2022, I contacted Estilita. She was 80 years old and lived in Costa Rica. I asked her about the group and she wrote that it included, "Ruby from Mexico; Ximena from Bolivia; Marisa, Mariusa and Sforza from Argentina; . . . Olcese from Brazil; Gloria, Cuban American; Ruth from Guatemala." Facebook direct message to author, January 5, 2022.

8. Alan Cartnal, "Salsa, the Symbol of a Latin Renaissance: Soul with a Spanish Accent," *L.A. Times*, January 16, 1977, page 49.

9. "Combahee River Collective: A Black Feminist Statement," *off our backs* 9, no. 6 (1979), p. 6–8.

10. Eighteen years later after I walked on to the jobsite, Loyola Marymount University took over what at the time was known as the former Hughes Aircraft Company's headquarters. They converted it to classrooms, faculty and administrative offices. See Brad Berton, "LMU to Take Over Hughes Headquarters," *L.A. Times*, January 11, 2000, p. 169.

CHAPTER 4

1. Gustavo Arellano, "Dodgers Pitcher Valenzuela Instilled Faith in a Generation," *L.A. Times*, April 7, 2021, p. A9. A different version of this article is available online at https://www.latimes.com/sports/dodgers/story/2021-04-07/fernando-valenzuela-fernandomania-religious-experience, accessed February 22, 2023.

2. There were a few Mikes in my class, so I have changed Mike Gonzales' name to "Tom" in this chapter, because I also mention another "Mike" known as "The Animal" in this chapter.

3. Cottontail Ranch closed in 2007; see Jaime Franklin, "Cottontail Ranch to Close Due to Economic Problems," *Pepperdine Graphics*, January 18, 2007 (http://pepperdine-graphic.com/cottontail-ranch-to-close-due-to-economic-problems/, accessed February 17, 2022).

4. N. Reiko Kato, "Lesbians of Color Conference: The Politics of 'Sisterhood,'" in *Voices of Color*, edited by Y. Alaniz and N. Wong, (Seattle: Red Letter Press, 1999): 30–34; Nancy Reiho Kato, "Lesbians of Color Conference: The Politics of 'Sisterhood,'" *Freedom Socialist Newspaper* 8, no. 4 (Winter 1983), available at https://socialism.com/fs-article/lesbians-of-color-conference-the-politics-of-sisterhood/ (accessed August 9, 2022).

5. As I conducted the research for this book, I learned that other gay Latino groups had organized in the LA area before GLLU. The ONE National Gay and Lesbian Archives holds a letter Rick Reyes wrote in 1972 claiming that his group had marched in the PRIDE Parade and had also sent a representative to the National Democratic Convention. The name of his group,

"Gavachos and Latinos Care," indicates that it was a white and Brown gay group. The Latinos subject file at the archive includes a flyer from Latinos Unidos, who came together in 1976. At one point, Latinos Unidos seemed to have had extensive programing. They issued a newsletter in which they stated that "solv[ing] problems unique to Gay Latin/Spanish Heritage men and women who expect to enjoy life" was one of their goals. This, coupled with a statement welcoming everyone to their group, indicates that building ethnic solidarity and pride was not at the top of Latinos Unidos' priorities. This is the extent of my knowledge of either group, because I had not heard about them while I was active in GLLU. See the Latinos subject file at the ONE National Gay and Lesbian Archives, USC Libraries, University of Southern California.

6. *LA Weekly*, January 6, 1983, p. 68.
7. Advertisement, *Progress Bulletin* (Pomona, California), February 14, 1975, p. 18.
8. See Natalia Molina, *A Place at the Nayarit: How a Mexican Restaurant Nourished a Community* (Berkeley: University of California Press, 2022) for a discussion of urban anchors. Molina considers business clientele a factor in accentuating the social networks evident in urban anchors; see page 63.
9. Some sources indicate that the photographs were taken in 1986, but I broke my hand early that year, on January 16, and I am clearly not wearing a cast in the photos.
10. The essays in Sybil Venegas and Rebecca Epstein's *Laura Aguilar: Show and Tell* (Los Angeles: UCLA Chicano Studies Research Center Press, 2017) explore Laura's photography in terms of its social, historical, and art-historical contexts. An interview with Christopher Velasco offers further insight into Laura Aguilar's art and life; see "A Conversation with the Laura Aguilar Trust" at https://www.youtube.com/watch?v=VCrBlPMWXlw, accessed February 28, 2023. As evidenced by my book cover, Laura also took photographs of me at other locations.
11. Richard T. Rodríguez, "Rebecca Epstein's Laura Aguilar: Show and Tell," in *Aztlan: A Journal of Chicano Studies* 43, no. 2 (Fall 2018): p. 314.
12. Karen Peterson, "Ry Cooder Pays Tribute to Lalo Guerrero, The Father of Chicano Music, at Centennial Birthday Concert," *Acoustic Guitar*, May 2017, https://acousticguitar.com/ry-cooder-pays-tribute-to-lalo-guerrero-the-father-of-chicano-music-at-centennial-birthday-concert/, accessed March 2, 2023. Also see Lalo Guerrero and Sherilyn Mentes, *Lalo: My Life and Music* (Tucson: University of Arizona Press, 2002).

CHAPTER 5

1. JSTOR is an online digital library available through most libraries that allows you to access to all the back issues of *off our backs*. According to JSTOR, "*off our backs* is a news journal by, for, and about women. It was published continuously from 1970 to 2008, making it the longest surviving feminist newspaper in the United States. It is run by a collective where all decisions are made by consensus."

2. Mujer a Mujer is briefly discussed in Thalia G. Kidder's "Networks in Transnational Labor Organizing" in *Restructuring World Politics: Transnational Social Movements, Networks, and Norms*, ed. by Sanjeev Khagram et al. (Minnesota: University of Minnesota Press, 2002), 281–283.

3. Lucinda Grinnell provides extensive information about women's groups and organizing in Mexico City. See "'Lesbianas Presente:' Lesbian Activism, Transnational Alliances, and the State in Mexico City, 1968–1991," dissertation, University of New Mexico, 2013. Some have reported that Mujer a Mujer organized the Encuentro, but although they may have been part of LAL, Mexicanas were the main organizers. See Teresa Carrillo, "Maria del Carmen de Lara," in *Talking Visions: Multicultural Feminism in a Transnational Age*, ed. by Ella Shohat (Cambridge: MIT Press, 2001), 402.

4. I mention Estilita Grimaldo in Chapter 3. In 1974 she organized the original Lesbianas Latina Americanas group in Los Angeles.

5. Later reports claimed that Mujer a Mujer or LAL "made funds available" for Latinas from the U.S. to attend the Encuentro. See Terresa Carrillo, "Maria del Carmen de Lara," page 402. I never heard a U.S. Latina mention that their travel expenses had been subsidized by Mujer a Mujer or LAL, but I did not know all the U.S. Latinas who attended. Much of the correspondence we received from LAL indicated a severe lack of fiscal resources. Like the other LU women, I saved for months to cover my travel expenses and registration fees of $80.00. A roundtrip ticket from L.A. to Mexico City cost around $250 at that time. LU held a special fundraiser at Kitty's, a club in East Los Angeles on September 26, 1987 that specifically raised money to defray costs for LU members to attend the Encuentro. LU raised $540. They also received $150 in donations. A total of $690 was split eight ways to help LU members attend the Encuentro. All other fundraising events and proceeds from the raffle went directly to LAL and toward supporting the Encuentro.

6. Yvonne Yarbro-Bejarano, "Primer Encuentro de Lesbianas Feministas Latinoamericanas y Caribeñas," in *Third Woman: The Sexuality of Latinas*

ed. by Norma Alarcón, Ana Castillo, and Cherríe Moraga (Berkeley: Third Woman Press,1993), 143–146.

7.   LU member Elena Popp wrote an extensive summary of the Encuentro. See "First Encuentro of Feminist Lesbians," *off our backs* 18, no 3 (March 1988): p. 32–33.

8.   The Latina Lesbian Support Group met at the El Centro Human Services, located at 972 S. Goodrich Boulevard. It had been started by Connexxus Women's Center/Centro de Mujeres, and LU took it over when Connexxus disbanded in 1990. I was GLLU President when LU took over the group. They managed it until 1994. At that point, El Centro Human Services took responsibility for keeping the support group going, but I am not sure how long they continued. For great insight on and interviews with Latinas who participated in the support group see, Robin Podolsky, "Creating Lesbian Communities," *LA Weekly*, June 29, 1989, p. 25. New queer scholarship has emerged, specifically focusing on East Los Angeles. One notable example is the work of Stacy I. Macías. See, "A Gay Bar, Some Familia, and Latina Butch-Femme: Rounding Out the Eastside Circle at El Monte's Sugar Shack," in *East of East: The Making of Greater El Monte*, ed. Romeo Guzmán, Carribean Fragoza, Alex Sayf Cummings, and Ryan Reft (Rutgers University Press, 2020), 250–260. Also see, Vicente Carrillo, "Pride Arrives to the Barrio: An Ethnographic Reflection of Boyle Heights' Orgullo Fest," April 6, 2022, in Latinx Talk: Research, Commentary, Creativity, accessed June 30, 2023, https://latinxtalk.org/2022/04/06/pride-arrives-to-the-barrio -an-ethnographic-reflection-of-boyle-heights-orgullo-fest/.

9.   For entertaining insight into the fire and library see, Susan Orlean, *The Library Book* (New York: Simon and Schuster, 2018).

10. Interestingly, the newspaper referred to me as "a 32-year-old gay Latina." See "Minorities: Homosexuals Are Still Struggling for Acceptance," *L.A. Times*, April 10, 1989, pt. 2, p. 14.

11. On April 30, 1988 I attended an ACT UP/LA protest and overnight vigil to demand LA/USC Hospital healthcare bureaucrats establish an AIDS ward. The L.A. County supervisors approved establishing a separate AIDS ward four months later; see Janny Scott and Victor Merina, "Supervisors Vote to Establish AIDS Ward at County-USC," *L.A. Times*, August 24, 1988, pt. 1, p. 28.

12. Morgan Gendel, "AIDS and 'An Early Frost': The Whisper Becomes a Shout," *L.A. Times*, November 13, 1985, pt. 6, p. 1.

13. Kai Ito, "Minorities' AIDS Help Insufficient, Officials Say: Cultural Gap, Funding Cited," *L.A. Times*, September 1, 1986, p. 27.

14. Carl Bean with David Ritz, *I Was Born This Way: A Gay Preacher's Journey through Gospel Music, Disco Stardom, and a Ministry in Christ* (New York: Simon and Schuster, 2013), 232.

15. "AIDS Increase," *Los Angeles Sentinel*, February 23, 1984, p. A10.

16. Sergio Muñoz, "With an Open Mind, L.A.'s Latino Community Must Prepare to Battle AIDS," *L.A. Times*, October 12, 1988, p. 27. Note that Muñoz chose to issue this call to action on October 12, which symbolizes the arrival of European colonization in the Americas.

17. Benita Roth, *The Life and Death of ACT UP/LA: Anti-AIDS Activism in Los Angeles from the 1980s to the 2000s* (Cambridge: Cambridge University Press, 2017). Also see Sarah Schulman's comprehensive and poignant book, *Let the Record Show: A Political History of ACT UP New York, 1987–1993* (New York: Farrar, Straus, and Giroux, 2021).

18. Steven A. Chin, "Huerta Attack Video Studied: Footage Shows UFW Leaders Hit at Bush Protest," *The San Francisco Examiner*, September 17, 1988, p. 2.

19. Robb Hernandez, *VIVA Records, 1970–2000: Lesbian and Gay Latino Artists of Los Angeles* (Los Angeles: UCLA Chicano Studies Research Center, 2013).

20. Gerald M. Boyd, "Reagan Urges Abstinence for Young to Avoid AIDS," *New York Times*, April 2, 1987, A13.

21. According to a 1987 U.S. Census estimate, Latinos made up 7.7% of the U.S. population yet accounted for 14% of the AIDS cases in September 1987. See Lanie Flores, "Warning on AIDS Aimed at Latinos," *L.A. Times*, October 13, 1987, p. 89. This article provides insight into the type of literature HIV/AIDS agencies were being funded to design and produce for Latinos. It features a photograph of a physician telling a terrified Latino man in Spanish, "AIDS, Mr. Jimenez, that terrible disease that affects the body's defenses, leaving it incapable of protecting itself against infections. I'm sorry sir, but as of yet, there is no cure." The article did not mention how much AIDS funding went towards producing this pamphlet, but it does mention that it was going to cost $2,500 to distribute and that APLA expected to spend another $30,000 to distribute it. Despite the tens of thousands being spent on HIV/AIDS literature and advertising campaigns, volunteer labor produced and distributed the GLLU brochure. Each printing cost $117.15.

22. I apologize to anyone whose name I left off this AIDS Advisory Board list. GLLU board members were always included as part of the group, as were Mario Solis-Marich, Eliseo Martinez, Veronica Flores, Eduardo Archuleta and Tomas Soto, who served as GLLU president after me.

23. *Transcript of Proceedings: National Commission on Acquired Immune Deficiency Syndrome* (Hollywood, January 25, 1990), in the National Com-

mission on AIDS, 1989–1993 collection on the National Library of Science website (https://profiles.nlm.nih.gov/101763264X61). My testimony can be found on pages 228–229.

CONCLUSION

1.   Tomm Carroll, "El Vez Lives: The Tongue-in-Check 'Mexican Elvis' Puts a Satirical Spin on The King," *News-Pilot* (San Pedro, California), September 6, 1991, p. 23.

2.   The earthquake occurred on January 17, 1994. See James Rainey, "Quake's Toll on Coliseum: $35 Million," *L.A. Times*, January 29, 1994, p. 1. Officials referred to the damage to the facility as "a disaster." Five months later, earthquake repairs soared to $58 million according to Kenneth Reich and Earl Gustkey's, "FEMA OK's More Funds for Quake Repairs at Coliseum," *L.A. Times*, July 29, 1994, B11. By this time, a workforce of 600–800 people worked around the clock on the project. The tight deadline and the large work force resulted in numerous accidents at the job site. Most were much more severe than mine.

3.   Carolina A. Miranda, "Laura Aguilar, 1959–2018: Chronicled Body, Chicano Identity," *L.A. Times*, April 27, 2018, B1.

4.   Ben Beaumont-Thomas, "Carl Bean, Singer of Gay Pride Anthem I Was Born This Way, Dies Aged 77," *The Guardian*, September 8, 2021, https://www.theguardian.com/music/2021/sep/08/carl-bean-singer-i-was-born-this-way-dies-aged-77, accessed April 15, 2023.

5.   Summer Lin, "L.A. County's Historic General Hospital is Set to be Converted into Affordable Housing," *L.A. Times*, July 27, 2022, https://www.latimes.com/california/story/2022-07-27/los-angeles-county-general-hospital-affordable-housing-project, accessed April 15, 2023.

6.   Learn more about Bienestar at https://www.bienestar.org/.

7.   One Archives Foundation, "Together on the Air," https://togetherontheair.onearchives.org/exhibit/listening-room-radio-gllu, accessed April 18, 2023.

8.   Lydia Otero, "My Archive: 20 Years of Los Angeles' LGBTQ+ Movement," *High Country News*, March 23, 2022, https://www.hcn.org/issues/54.4/south-history-my-archive-20-years-of-los-angeles-lgbtq-movement, accessed April 18, 2023.

APPENDIX

Gallery of Additional Images

FIGURE A.1 Lesbiana Latina Americanas Flyer, 1980. Created by author. "Latinas" File at ONE Institute, Los Angeles.

Workshop Series on Horizontal Hostility

Lesbians of Color
Lesbianas Latinas Americanas

August 1980

Notes by EMMA PÉREZ

Description/Statement of Purpose

The term lateral racism has seemed to be the most common-
ly applied to the problems between our cultures. However racism
implies power and therefore is not applicable to us as women of
color. In coming up with a more appropriate name such terms as
cultural oppression and lateral oppression were suggested. Flo
Kennedy (black feminist activist) coined the term horizontal
hostility. Spelled out it speaks of our lateral oppression of
each other because we cannot reach the real enemy. It is meant
to provoke extensive thought as to the nature and effects of
this type of oppression.

Oppress. 1. To subjugate or persecute by unjust use of force
or authority. 2. To weigh heavily upon, especially so as to
depress the mind or spirits. 3. To overwhelm or crush.
Oppression. 1. That which oppresses or burdens. 2. A feeling of being heavily weighed down, either mentally or physically;
depression; weariness.
Oppressive. 1. Difficult to bear; harsh; tyrannical. 2. Causing a state of physical or mental distress.

The roots of horizontal hostility is white racism. There is
an ever present need for us as committed lesbians of color to
examine the effects white racism has had upon us. We are a society
based on cast. Those who see addressing the issue of horizontal hostility as vital, as our only means of survival and as
a positive growth experience, will come together for a minimum
of four weeks to begin breaking through these oppressive attitudes. We recognize that horizontal hostility does stem from
white racism but that we do in fact adopt many of their attitudes
and standards, thereby oppressing each other. If we as lesbians
of color do not unify ourselves in the truest sense we will
certainly kill each other off, saving our racist structure (the
white man) the trouble. We cannot hope to influence or teach
the masses unless we recognize ourselves as a part of that mass.
We will help each other in recognizing the tactics that have
successfully divided us within our own cultures as well as others.
During a process of information sharing and honest disclosure we will begin learning about ourselves and our cultures
as well as sorting through our attitudes, placing them into
their proper perspective.
These workshops are not set up to be a dialogue between
latinas and black women per se. Latinas actually represent
many cultures and will not always agree nor will black women
have the same perspective all of the time. Each women will be
encouraged to express her feelings honestly.

FIGURE A.2 Page 1 of LOC and La Las Horizontal Hostility Workshops, 1980.
Courtesy of Emma M. Pérez.

Statement of Purpose (con't)

By the end of the four weeks we hope to have come an important step closer to uniting as a strong, effective and loving
unit, taking pride in being connected by blood.

Structure - Physical Breakdown

1. Ideally there will be 8-10 women per group. Each group
will have a facilitator who's role is to insure a smooth flow,
keeping group process as free of   try to
difficulties or obstacles as possible. She will also stimulate
and aid in the flow of conversation, disclosure, revelation, etc..
Each woman has her own individual style, her own uniqueness
and should feel comfortable in her style of communicating. Everyone is expected however, to respect her sisters. If it were to
happen that two sisters have unresolvable conflict and it gets
to the point of disrespect,stagnation,physical confrontation,
assuming the facilitator has tried all else, she reserves the right
to then ask the woman/women to leave the group until the following
week. This measure was suggested as a precaution against volatile
situations have occured in other workshops, causing the group to
become ineffective. Hopefully this will not happen. If and when
the going gets rough we will act responsibly and with caring.
2. There will be 2-3 groups depending on the number of
women that sign up. Each group will meet for four (4) consecu-
tive weeks.
3. Once the groups are formed and the first meeting is held
they will be closed to newcomers from then on. This is to maintain
an environment of trust and intimacy.
4. We will meet each Sunday beginning August 10, 1980 from
4:00 - 7:00 P.M.. For the first 10-15 minutes of each workshop
both groups will come together for an update, information sharing and general exchange.
5. The last 30 minutes will concentrate on individual group
closure. The focus will be summary of accomplishment, resolve,
where to pick up the following week, etc..
6. On the 4th week (August 31) all groups will merge. It
is here that we will decide the future of these workshops. We
will discuss what we've achieved and what it is we have not. Goals,
Our feelings about the past 3 weeks, about each other and ourselves.
A sharing of personal experience. It's possible that we may
want or need to pick up unfinished discussion. We want to realize
our potential. Now is also the best time for stressing our
commonalities, our bonds and committments, our dreams and visions
as third world lesbians.
7. For week 5 Matu has suggested a potluck. Since everybody likes parties then everyone is invited to bring their favorite
home-cooked, ethnic dish. Turkey franks also accepted. We'll
have the party/potluck at someone's home so volenteers come forth
and let's boogie!!

FIGURE A.3 Page 2 of LOC and La Las Horizontal Hostility Workshops, 1980.
Courtesy of Emma M. Pérez.

1983 National Lesbians of Color Conference
1983 Conferencia Nacional de Lesbianas de Color

Thursday - Sunday
September 8 - 11,
1983

de Jueves a Domingo
Septiembre 8 - 11,
1983

Sisters Bonding Together
Hermanas Unidas

Cottontail Ranch in Malibu, California
Cabins and tent spaces are available

Rancho Cottontail en Malibu, California
Cabañas y espacio para casas de campaña son disponibles

Seminars and Workshops in:
• Education
• Politics
• Health
• Spirituality
• Culture

Seminarios y Talleres en:
• Educación
• Política
• Salúd
• Espiritualidad
• Cultura

Plus: Art, Music, Poetry, and Dance

Además: Artes, Música, Poesia, y Baile

Join with lesbians of color from all over the country as we explore ways to work together and grow stronger.

Únase con lesbianas de color de todas partes del país para explorar maneras de trabajar juntas y acernos más fuertes.

Conference Cost $75
(includes food, accommodations, and registration)
Low Income $60
Children $35
(boys must be 12 or under)
Donations Welcomed (to help someone else come)

Costo de la Conferencia $75
(incluye comida, comodidades, y registración)
Sueldo Bajo $60
Niños $35
(niños masculinos deben tener bajo de 12 años de edad)
Donaciones son Bienvenidas (para ayudar que otra mujer pueda venir)

Advance Registration required by July 12, 1983. Please register early as space is limited. Send your Non-Refundable Deposit of $30 with your Registration Form (applies towards total conference cost).

Registración Avanzada es requerida antes del 12 de Julio 1983. Por favor registrese temprano, como el espacio es limitado. Mande su Depósito de $30 (cual no se restituye) con su Forma de Registración. El Depósito se aplica a su costo total de la conferencia.

For more information, special needs, or late registration write:
Para más información, asistencia especial, ó registración tarde escriba a:

Lesbians of Color/Lesbianas de Color
P.O. Box 2344

Registration Form / Forma de Registración

Name / Nombre

Address / Dirección

City / Ciudad   State / Estado   Zip

FIGURE A.4 1983 National LOC Conference poster. Private collection of author.

"I know the Conference is a tremendous undertaking. The dream of a National Lesbian of Color Conference has lived in my visions for more years that I can tell you, and the fact that you are making it real is a wonderful, inspiring and generative act. And remember, this one is only the first. We will not be able to do everything in it, but the fact of its existence is herstoric. Please tell the women that my heart's energies will be with you, and my loving spirit, since I can't be there in person. If we can see each other's face clearly, and use our differences as arches joining our common efforts, as torches illuminating those we may not share, then we will move toward that strength that means success in all things. And remember, it will not be easy, learning one another's powers, learning one another's fears. But we must do it, or perish into what the others wish us to be, each other's destroyer. And of course we do not want to become that, nor to do our enemies' work for them. Love and courage and persistence."

                                                                    Audre Lorde

— 3 —

FIGURE A.5 Message from Audre Lorde in the National LOC Conference Program, 1983. Private collection of author.

FIGURE A.6 Gloria Anzaldúa at National LOC Conference, 1983. Photograph by author.

FIGURE A.7 Large gathering at National LOC Conference, 1983. Photograph by author.

LETTERS TO THE EDITOR

A SPECIAL MESSAGE FROM CESAR CHAVEZ TO
GLLU UPON THE OCCASION OF THEIR SECOND
ANNIVERSARY

Estimados Compañeros y Compañeras:

Dear Editor:

Analizing the article that appeared in
the L.A. Herald Examiner of October 23,
1983, I came to the conclusion that the
reporter, Rubén Castañeda , only presented
one side on the coin in his treatment of
the Gay/Lesbian Latino/a Community. He
presented a masculine orientation with
heterosexist implications.

It was obvious that through out the entire article Mr. Castañeda underestimated
the value of the Lesbian Latina experience
For example, he ignored the co-sexual reality that exists in our population by
choosing a masculine terminology for the
main title of the article.*

This "lesbiphobic" attitude persists
throughout the entire article. It can be
found in the pictures, where he choose to
present Gay men only. There was also a
significant imbalance in the quantity and
context of the interviews. He presented
6 Gay men and only 1 Lesbian.

Rubén Castañeda continued the tradi-
tional idea that the man is the "political
animal" and the woman is the "sexual
object." He chose positive characteris-
tics to describe Gays, such as being capable of leadership, power, and activism.
With the Lesbians he limited himself to
presenting their physical aspect only. By
the way that he described the Lesbians, I
perceived his sexual appetite for one, and
how he used negative stereotypes for the
ones the he disapproved of. For example,
his saying that they look like "the female
version of Mr. T," I feel, as a Lesbian
Latina, that, for Rubén Castañeda , we
Lesbians are not capable of performing
duties or sharing in the struggle with our
fellow Gay men.

I think that with his article he brings
a new issue to surface our community,
creating barriers of separatism, which we,
with so much of our effort, are trying to
overcome.

Thank you,
Eileen Pagán

*"Gay Hispanics in L.A. Face Double
Jeopardy."

It is always a privilege to be with you,
though at times it has to be through an
emissary. It is a privilege first because
there seems to be a special bond between
groups whose people struggle for liberation, human dignity, and a rightful share
of the abundance of this planet, but I
think even more so because we are from
each other, and as we celebrate this special day, the sixteenth of September, we
congratulate you on your second anniversary. Congratulations are in order because you aren't just another Hispanic
group that has organized to simply do nothing. We have watched you and applauded
your tremendous organizing energy. We
have gratefully observed your spirit and
discipline on our boycott picket lines.

And during Gay Pride Week when our leadership marched with you in Los Angeles, we
saw the overwhelming evidence of the enthusiastic support you have organized for
La Causa among Southern California's Gay
and Lesbian communitites. We are grateful
for all you have done for us; we salute
your dedicated leadership, including two
very special proteges of La Causa: Frank
Mendiola and Conrado Terrazas; we encourage you to continue in your efforts to
organize to help yourselves, as well as
those who are still at the very bottom of
the nation's economy, the farm workers;
and we wish you the success you deserve
in your efforts to form a strong national
organization. Maintain your spirit of
selflessness and we know that you will
succeed.

¡Si se puede!   -César E. Chávez
                    President, U.F.W.

FIGURE A.8 Letter from César Chávez to GLLU. *Unidad*, December/January, 1984.

TO: ALL OUR SISTERS

FROM: GAY & LESBIAN LATINOS UNIDOS

GAY & LESBIAN LATINOS UNIDOS WAS CREATED TO EDUCATE BOTH THE GAY/LESBIAN
LATINO COMMUNITY AND THE GENERAL PUBLIC ABOUT THE OPPRESSIONS SUFFERED
BY GAY AND LESBIAN LATINOS.

OUR GOALS ARE TO HELP ELIMINATE NEGATIVE GAY/LESBIAN LATINO STEREOTYPES,
RACISM, CLASSISM, HOMOPHOBIA, AND SEXISM WITHIN -- AND OUTSIDE -- OUR
GAY/LESBIAN COMMUNITY. WE ARE COMMITTED TO PROMOTING A POSITIVE SELF-
IMAGE FOR GAY/LESBIAN LATINOS; TO DEFEND THE CIVIL AND HUMAN RIGHTS OF ALL
GAY/LESBIAN LATINOS; TO ELEVATE THE CULTURAL AND ECONOMIC DEVELOPMENT OF
THE GAY/LESBIAN LATINO COMMUNITY; AND TO UNITE THE GAY/LESBIAN LATINO
COMMUNITY.

GAY & LESBIAN LATINOS UNIDOS "GENERAL ASSEMBLY" MEETINGS ARE HELD THE
2ND THURSDAY OF EVERY MONTH, AT 7:30 PM, IN THE GAY & LESBIAN COMMUNITY
SERVICES CENTER (1213 N. HIGHLAND AVE./HOLLYWOOD). OUR "ORIENTATION"
MEETINGS ARE HELD THE 4TH THURSDAY OF EVERY MONTH (SAME TIME & LOCATION).
PLEASE CALL: (213) 464-7400 / EXT. 434 FOR MORE INFORMATION.

OUR STRENGTH LIES IN OUR UNITY. AND OUR UNITY DEPENDS ON OUR PRIDE --
FOR OURSELVES AND EACH OTHER. WE ARE LATINO/A. WE ARE GAY AND LESBIAN.

WE ARE ONE.

FIGURE A.9   GLLU Outreach to Lesbians, 1983. Private collection of author.

The Lesbians of Gay and Lesbian Latinos Unidos sponsor "Sharing Our Historias"

series of raps at the Gay and Lesbian Community Services Center, 1213 N. Highland Avenue, L.A., (213)464-7400 ext 434 Geneva or ext.246, Jay Jay

One: "Coming Out to La Familia" - May 21st, 6-8pm, meet at the Center lobby.

Two: "The Chicana Experience" (open to all Latina lesbians) - June 25th, 6-8 p.m., Rm. 207.

Three: "Católicas" (open to gay Latinos)- July 24rd, 8 - 10 p.m., Rm. 203

Four: "Dinero:¿Que es la importancia?/Classism"-Aug.28th, 8 - 10 p.m., Rm. 203.

Five: "Latinas: Avenues for Community Involvement" - Sept. (date, time and place announced at prior mtgs)

Six: "Lesbian Vision/Vista del Futuro"-Oct. (date, time and place announced at prior mtgs.)

As a committee of G.L.L.U., the Lesbianas (Lesbian Task Force) serve as a support group for Latinas. This is meant to encourage more lesbian participation within G.L.L.U. It is also a means to address the specific issues and needs of Latinas.

FIGURE A.10 Lesbian Task Force (before changing their name to LU) flyer announcing rap groups, 1984. "Lesbianas Unidas" File, ONE Institute in Los Angeles.

FIGURE A.11 Smaller GLLU banner designed to show solidarity with the Central American struggle and people around 1983. Photograph by Louis Jacinto.

FIGURE A.12 Tommy performing during Cultural Night at the GLLU Retreat in 1984. Photograph by Louis Jacinto.

FIGURE A.13 GLLU at Pride around 1983. Photograph by Louis Jacinto.

FIGURE A.14 GLLU at Pride around 1984. Photograph by Louis Jacinto.

FIGURE A.15 LU Cultural Night performance at 1986 LU Retreat. Left to right: Author, Irene, Anna Maria and Carmen. Private collection of author.

FIGURE A.16 Cultural Night performance at 1986 LU Retreat. Left to right: Author, Irene and Anna Maria. Private collection of author.

THE
NATIONAL JOINT APPRENTICESHIP AND TRAINING
COMMITTEE FOR THE ELECTRICAL INDUSTRY

Certificate of Completion of Apprenticeship

This Certificate of Completion of Apprenticeship is awarded to

Lydia Otero

and certifies the successful completion of apprenticeship in accordance with the National Standards
formulated and approved by the National Joint Apprenticeship and Training Committee for the
Electrical Industry, in cooperation with the Federal Committee on Apprenticeship.

Presented this **eighth** day of **November, 1986**

in the City of **Los Angeles**

Joint Apprenticeship and   National Joint Apprenticeship and Training
Training Committee   Committee for the Electrical Industry

_____   _____
                 Chairman   International President, IBEW, and Co-chairman, NJATC

_____   _____
                 Secretary   Vice President, NECA, and Co-chairman, NJATC

FIGURE A.17   Author's completion of apprenticeship, 1986. Private collection of author.

GAY and LESBIAN LATINOS UNIDOS

1213 N. Highland Ave
Hollywood, CA 90038

July 24, 1987

Queridas Hermanas:

As many of you know the Primer Encuentro de Lesbianas
Femenistas Latinoamericanas y Caribenas is set to take place on
October 14, 15, 16 and 17, 1987 near Mexico City. On Saturday,
August 1, 1987, Barbara Yllam, a member of the organizing
committee, will be in Los Angeles to give us the latest update on
the Encuentro. Lesbianas Unidas would like to assure that all of
you who are planning to attend the Encuentro have an opportunity
to meet and talk with Barbara. She is making this special trip
to encourage Latina lesbians from the Los Angeles area to attend
the Encuentro. The latest word from the organizers is that <u>all</u>
Latina lesbians who are interested in attending will be welcome
at the Encuentro. So don't miss your chance to get all the
latest details.

Our regular monthly meeting which was scheduled for
Saturday, August 8, 1987, is now re-scheduled for Saturday,
August 1, 1987 at 5:30 p.m. at Estilita Grimaldo's house, 5314 N.
Figueroa in Highland Park. The directions to Estilita's house
are as follows: Take the Pasadena Freeway, North; exit on
Avenue 52 and turn left; on Figueroa turn right and it is on the
right hand side, where it says Womantours. Estilita's phone
number is (213) 255-1115.

We apologize for not letting you know sooner about the new
date for our meeting, but we just found out that Barbara was
going to be in Los Angeles next weekend.

We hope that many of you will take advantage of this
opportunity to meet Barbara and to discuss your travel
arrangements with Estilita, our official travel agent for the
Encuentro.

Un abrazo,

CARLA BARBOZA,
Secretary, Lesbianas Unidas

FIGURE A.18 Letter from LU regarding the Encuentro, 1986. Private collection
of author.

all womens event

SINIGUAL
WOMENS   IS   SALSA
          HERE

AUGUST 15, 1987

FRIENDSHIP AUDITORIUM
3201 RIVERSIDE DRIVE
LOS ANGELES

TICKETS AVAILABLE AT

champagne
reception   8–9 p.m

dance   9–1 a.m   dance only
    $15.00 $12.50

no one turned away for lack of funds

sponsored by lesbianas unidas(g.l.l.u) and connexxus

Connexxus(213) 859-3960

Sisterhood Bookstore/Westwood
        (213) 477-7300

A Different Light/Silverlake(213) 668-0629

Page One/ Pasadena(818) 798-8694

or at the door

for further info:(213) 250–0812

FIGURE A.19 Flyer for the Sinigual event, 1987. Private collection of author.

FIGURE A.20 U.S. Latinas meeting at the Encuentro in Cuernavaca, 1986. Photograph by Laura Aguilar. Courtesy of the Laura Aguilar Trust.

FIGURE A.21 U.S. Latinas meeting at the Encuentro in Cuernavaca, author (center) 1986. Photograph by Laura Aguilar. Courtesy of the Laura Aguilar Trust.

FIGURE A.22 Example of Mike Garcia's artwork created for GLLU. Private collection of author.

First National Latina Lesbian CONFERENCE

De diferentes raices..... de diferentes madres.....
Somos Hermanas.

SEPTEMBER 3 - 5, 1988
Labor Day Weekend
in
Los Angeles , California

GOALS: 1) To provide an opportunity for Latina Lesbians from across the country to meet, **network**, get to know each other and learn from each other;
        2) To establish a **National Latina Lesbian organization** that will facilitate on-going national networking;
        3) To provide a place where Latina Lesbians can **gather annually or semi-annually**; where we can hear each other's stories, do away with the isolation we sometimes feel, and garner strength to do the work we do in our own communities;
        4) To enlarge and strengthen the **political power** we have as Latina Lesbians through education, sharing information, and by increasing our visibility;

ORGANIZED BY
LESBIANAS UNIDAS
OF Gay and Lesbian Latinos Unidos
1213 N. HIGHLAND AVENUE
HOLLYWOOD, CA 90038

From different roots.... and different wombs....we are SISTERS.

FIGURE A.23 LU Flyer for a National Conference (front), 1988. Private collection of author.

FIGURE A.24 Food preparation at LU Retreat around 1987. Private collection of author.

FIGURE A.25 Large meeting session at LU Retreat around 1988. Private collection of author.

FIGURE A.26 LU Retreat activity around 1989. Private collection of author.

FIGURE A.27 LU Cultural Night performance around 1989. Susana Brito (bongos) and Carmen Canto (guitar).

FIGURE A.28 Author speaking at Tom Bradley for Mayor rally around 1989. Private collection of author.

FIGURE A.29 Bevan Dufty, Gloria Molina and author at a Molina fundraiser, 1990. Private collection of author.

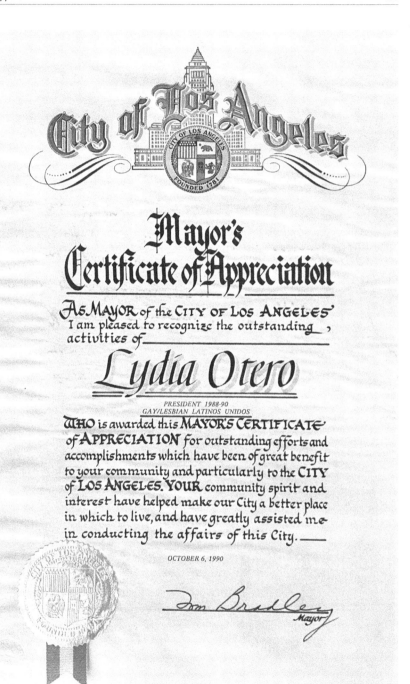

FIGURE A.30 Author's Certificate of Appreciation from Mayor Tom Bradley, 1990. Private collection of author.

FIGURE A.31 GLLU and LU around 1989. Private collection of author.

FIGURE A.32 GLLU and LU around 1990. Private collection of author.

GLLU ANNUAL CHRISTMAS TOY DRIVE

Date: December 16, 1989

Time: 6:00 p.m. to 12:00 a.m.

Place: 2628 West Avenue 35
Los Angeles 90065
(213) 663-0865
(213) 259-9989

Help us demonstrate the spirit of giving during this holiday season
by bringing an unwrapped toy or donation of $5.00.   These toys are
needed and will be greatly appreciated..

This year's toy drive will benefit the children of El Centro del Pueblo
from Echo Park, Parra Los Ninos from L.A.'s Skid Row and Rue's
House, a shelter for women and children with AIDS.

Please join us in celebrating the holiday and contributing to a most
worthy cause!

For your enjoyment, food and a no-host bar will be provided.

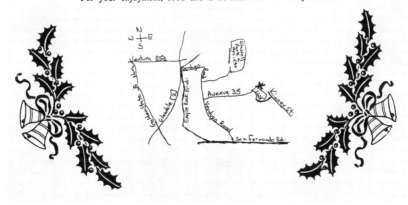

FIGURE A.33   GLLU Toy Drive Flyer, 1989. Private collection of author.

FIGURE A.34 GLLU Members holding banner at a Pride event around 1989. Left to right: Valentino Sandoval, Ted Salaises, Michael Puente and Eduardo Archuleta. Photograph by Louis Jacinto.

FIGURE A.35 Eduardo Archuleta (front) and Carlos Alvarado (back) at the first Bienestar office at Sunset Junction, 1989. Photograph by Louis Jacinto.

G.L.L.U

July 25, 1990

Robert E. Frangenberg
Director, AIDS Program
Department of Health Services
600 South Commonwealth, 6th Floor
Los Angeles, CA 90005

Dear Mr. Frangenberg:

Gay and Lesbian Latinos Unidos (GLLU) is proud to present the enclosed funding proposal program to the Department of Health Services. GLLU is a not-for-profit organization, established since 1981, working for the empowerment of the Latino gay and lesbian community in Los Angeles County regarding issues directly impacting their quality of life. We are currently the largest Latino gay and lesbian organization in the United States and are centrally located in the heart of the Latino gay and lesbian Los Angeles community.

The enclosed proposal describes our proposal for development of educational/prevention material on HIV/AIDS for gay and bisexual Latino men who are at high risk and who are HIV infected. GLLU currently provides secondary information and sees to expand by providing intervention/educational. The format by which GLLU proposes to increase practical knowledge about HIV /AIDS in the Latino gay community is by developing material that is Latino and gay culturally sensitive. It will provide basic and appropriate educational/prevention information, and will distinguish itself from other agencies that have developed such material. A distinction is that Bienestar's staff is Latino gay and bilingual/ bicultural which is culturally sensitive when developing such material. More importantly, the variety of educational/prevention services all ready being provided at Bienestar will compliment such booklets and can be of greater

Gay and Lesbian Latinos Unidos
P.O. Box 85459
Los Angeles, CA 90072

FIGURE A.36 Application for funding for Bienestar, 1990 (page 1). Private collection of author.

assistance to those who first know about Bienestar through the booklets or advertisements.

As detailed throughout the proposal, in Los Angeles County, gay and bisexual Latinos have become the population which is "falling through the cracks" of the AIDS education and service delivery sector. Latino gay and bisexual men may hesitate to access educational/prevention services at mainstream gay AIDS service organizations or Latino organizations with a broad target to serve. The Bienestar project provides gay and bisexual Latino men a safe, confidential, and non-judgemental environment in which to receive critically needed information. Furthermore, educational/prevention services will be provided by a staff with which participants can self identify themselves with and are sensitive to their needs.

The proposal request $ 39,529.00 for one year to provide awareness of HIV transmission, safe sex behavior, and testing (HIV) through prevention/ education material. Funding requested for these educational/prevention services are minimal when comparing it to the overall quality service that will be provided throughout the grant period.

We hope you will give our proposal your fullest consideration. If you need any additional information, please contact Lydia Otero at (213) 660-9681 or by writing to P.O. Box 85459, Los Angeles, CA 90072. On behalf of the Board of Directors of Gay and Lesbian Latinos Unidos, thank you for the opportunity to submit this proposal.

Sincerely,

Lydia Otero.
President, Board of Directors
Gay and Lesbian Latinos Unidos

FIGURE A.37 Application for funding for Bienestar, 1990 (page 2). Private collection of author.

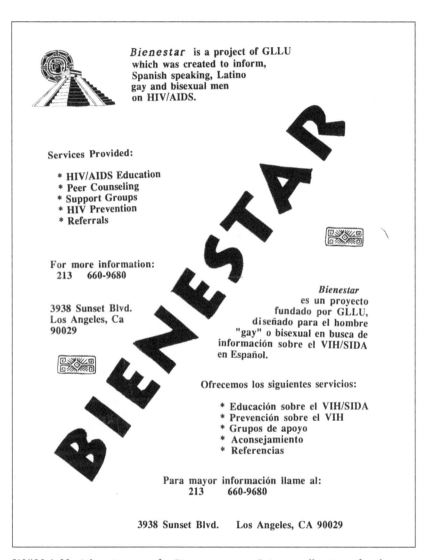

FIGURE A.38   Advertisement for Bienestar, 1990. Private collection of author.

January 2, 1990

Happy New Year Members and Supporters !!

This year holds many challenges for all of us in GLLU. We finally received AIDS funding at the end of last year but now comes the difficult part of implementing the programs and being accountable to funding agencies. This is the responsibility of the Board and we are spending much of our time on it, but even though AIDS is a priority we all know there is much more to GLLU. Thus this year we are going to have to depend even more on our committees to accomplish the goals of GLLU. If you are not active in a committee I encourage you to join and become involved because we need you to help this organization continue to be diverse, interesting, to voice concerns about our communities, and to move forward together.

General Assembly is on Thursday, January 11 at 7:30 at the Gay and Lesbian Services Center, 1213 N. Highland. We will elect someone to fill the new Board position, Programs Administrator that was created last meeting. The guest speakers for the meeting will be from GLAAD, an organization that GLLU has been working with in the last year. They are doing very good work in the community and we will get an opportunity to meet the co-chairs. Join us and invite any new Latinos and Latinas to check us out.

On a personal note, I would like to extend my thanks for your support last year. I think we had a good year, our events were successful, we have many new faces active in GLLU, and many people wanted to be on the board during elections in September. I think this is a good sign that individuals want to give to the organization, be part of the growth and make the commitment to be responsible and involved.

I encourage each of you to voice your opinions and ideas. Sometimes meetings are busy, and if you should ever feel you would like to talk to me about an idea feel free to call me. My phone number is (213) 664-4634.

Remember that saying from the 60's, " If you are not part of the solution you are part of the problem"

Lydia Otero
President

Gay and Lesbian Latinos Unidos
P.O. Box 85459
Los Angeles, CA 90072

FIGURE A.39 Letter from author to GLLU membership, 1990. Private collection of author.

G.L.L.U

June 26, 1990

Genevieve G. López
Director, Community Outreach Services
El Centro Human Services Corp.
972 Goodrich Blvd.
Los Angeles, CA 90022

Dear Genevieve:

I am writing to you as a Representative of G.L.L.U. to inform you of the status of the Latina Lesbian Support Group (LLSG). As you know Connexxus who formally sponsored the support groups will cease to operate at the end of June. Despite this, the LLSG decided to end its affiliation with Connexxus and to continue meeting on Mondays and Wednesdays from 7:00pm to 9:00pm under the sponsorship of Lesbianas Unidas a Committee of Gay and Lesbian Latinos Unidos (GLLU). This means that the support groups will now be operated and maintained by Lesbianas Unidas. The support group participants have unanimously agreed that we would like to continue meeting at El Centro and we are requesting approval to do so. We appreciate the support El Centro has shown us and hope to continue the relationship. At this time we have no operating budget and cannot offer "rental" payment. If this needs negotiation please contact me. The groups will be facilitated by volunteers, including myself, and as you know I have been the volunteer Facilitator/Coordinator of the group for the past year and a half.

Again, Genevieve, all that we require to continue the support groups will be a meeting room two (2) nights a week from 7:00pm to 9:00pm (four hours a week). If you have further questions I have enclosed my card so that you may contact me.

We thank you Genevieve for the past support you have demonstrated toward our group and hopefully for your continued support. We anticipate a response to our request.

Sincerely,

Irene Martinez
Board-Member/Special Projects
and Lesbianas Unidas of GLLU

Gay and Lesbian Latinos Unidos
P.O. Box 85459
Los Angeles, CA 90072

FIGURE A.40 Letter from LU regarding East L.A. Support Group, 1990. Irene Martínez and Laura Duran Collection.

GAY AND LESBIAN LATINOS UNIDOS

will march in the 20th anniversary of the

1990 NATIONAL
CHICANO MORATORIUM

Chicano Mexicano Self-determination

MARCH & RALLY

AUGUST 25, 1990

We will assemble at 9:00 a.m. at Albert Diaz Plaza (Belvedere Park)
in East Los Angeles and march to Salazar Park for a rally

What is the Chicano Moratorium? 20 years ago on August 27, 1970
twenty thousand people of all backgrounds marched peacefully in
the streets of East Los Angeles to protest the unusually high
number of Chicanos killed in Viet Nam, and the injustices of
Chicanos at home, such as low paying jobs, inadequate education,
poor housing, and medical care. This peaceful demonstration was
brutally interrupted by a police incited riot that killed 3
people including Ruben Salazar, a well know L.A. Times reporter,
injured countless others and hundreds were arrested. It is now
20 years later and little has changed for most
Chicanos/Mexicanos. Gay and Lesbian Latinos Unidos (GLLU) will
march along side thousands of others in commemoration of this
historical event and to renew our commitment to the renaissance
of the new Chicano/Mexicano movement. As Gay and Lesbian
Latino/as it is our right and responsibility to proclaim our
identities and our demands for a better life for all Latino/as.
We invite you to join us in East Los Angeles. Look for our
banner.

QUE VIVA LA RAZA!

FIGURE A.41 GLLU 1990 Chicano Moratorium Flyer. Private collection of author.

ABOUT THE AUTHOR

L.A. Interchanges is Lydia Otero's second memoir. The first, *In the Shadows of the Freeway: Growing Up Brown & Queer* (2019), recounts how urban development influenced formative aspects of their childhood. It also examines the multiple effects of intergenerational trauma and environmental racism. In *Notitas: Select Columns from the Tucson Citizen* (2021), Otero's book compilation features columns by Alva B. Torres, one of Tucson's most formidable activists who resisted the destruction that targeted barrios in the late 1960s. Otero's earliest book, *La Calle: Spatial Conflicts and Urban Renewal in a Southwestern City* (2010) focused on a 1966 urban renewal project, which targeted the most densely populated 80 acres in Arizona. Although Mexican Americans dominated the renewal area demographically, most of the city's Asian and African American residents also lived there.

The author has a Ph.D. in History and was a tenured professor in the Department of Mexican American Studies at the University of Arizona. They live in Tucson and remain deeply connected with Los Angeles through friends and family. (Photo by Maureen Campesino)